# THERE'S A PONY IN THAT CAR

**JAY GILBERT**

# There's a *Pony* in that Car!

## By
## JAY GILBERT

**Copyright © 2019 Jay Gilbert.**

First printing edition 2019

Second printing edition 2023

All rights reserved. No part of this publication may be reproduced, distributed, or transmitted in any form or by any means, including photocopying, recording, or other electronic or mechanical methods, without the prior written permission of the publisher, except in the case of brief quotations embodied in critical reviews and certain other noncommercial uses permitted by copyright law.

Contact the author: gilbertjay58@gmail.com

Cover and formatting by Paradox Book Cover & Formatting

# DEDICATION

*to John & Nancy Gilbert*

# CONTENTS

| | |
|---|---|
| Manhattans-n-Milk | 1 |
| A Bit of Background | 2 |
| Swan Lake | 6 |
| A Sunday Drive | 9 |
| There's a Pony in that Car | 12 |
| Living Nativity | 20 |
| Animal Farm | 29 |
| Ted the Attack Chicken | 34 |
| Chicken Plucking | 38 |
| Girls and Hay Bales | 46 |
| The Hay Box Horror | 51 |
| Burned Apples | 56 |
| The Talk | 62 |
| Who-He-Ha | 68 |
| Shower Time | 73 |
| The Everything Can | 77 |
| The Electric Fence Dance | 86 |
| Planting Ducks | 91 |
| Oh My Gosh Winnibigosh | 96 |
| Dukie Cakes | 107 |
| Deadheads | 113 |
| Ice Fishing | 119 |
| And Other Frozen Fun | 126 |
| Pussyfooting | 130 |
| Never Name Your Food | 134 |
| Hatchet Job | 137 |
| 1. Author's Note | 143 |
| Salties | 145 |
| Acknowledgments | 157 |
| Note From The Author | 158 |

About the Author 161
Also by Jay Gilbert 163

# MANHATTANS-N-MILK

December 31, 1958. My father had come down to the hospital to check on his newborn son (me) and Mom. He had snuck in a jigger of Manhattans for the new moms to celebrate New Year's Eve. Saint Luke's was a Catholic hospital. A nun came into the room on her rounds. She smelled the liquor, looked around the room, but couldn't find it and left. Once the coast was clear, Dad gave each mom a bump and left for the evening. Later the babies were brought in for their evening breastfeeding and returned to the nursery. All the babies that had Manhattan milk slept through the entire night.

## A BIT OF BACKGROUND

I had the honor and privilege of being raised by two of the most interesting people in the world. At least to me they were, and yes, I've met many people from all around the world. They all take a backseat to John Doucette and Nancy Ann Gilbert. Dad was known as "JD" to his friends, and lovingly as the "crazy Frenchman," or "Curly" by our mother. Later in life, we would call him "The Old Man." This is a term of endearment and respect in the South, where we would eventually land as a family.

Mom was an only child. Her father, Fred Montgomery, died when she was a little girl. Her mother, Irene, was an independent woman, who was not interested in getting remarried to provide for Nancy and herself. She went to work for a local paper box company as a bookkeeper.

To keep Nancy occupied, she signed her up for tap dancing lessons. Later, Mom would travel to Chicago to dance in shows. A voracious reader and talker, Nancy always loved a good party and entertaining. Lily-white skin, dark hair, and less than a hundred pounds dripping wet when she met Dad, Mom had great "gams," as they used to say.

Nancy loved her big family of boys. She always said, "boys are easier than girls...no drama." She relished planning birthday parties, cooking Thanksgiving turkeys so big Dad had a hard time getting them out of the roasting pan, and of course, Christmastime. The eternal optimist, Mom's glass was always half full. Always smiling and laughing out loud, she was plain fun to be around. As an only child, all she ever wanted was a big family. Boy, did she get one!

Dad was a man's man. An outdoorsman, he loved hunting, fishing, and trapping. He taught his boys by example, got things done, provided for his family, and never complained or whined about his work or station in life. Standing about five eight and weighing in at a lean, muscular hundred sixty pounds, he was as strong as an ox. With thick curly hair combed straight back and that French skin that always looked tan, to us kids he was larger than life. He was our real-life Paul Bunyan.

While naturally inclined to be in the great

outdoors or working around our little farm, JD could turn on the charm and be the life of any party. He had so many stories and such great delivery; he could very well have been a successful standup comedian. It was mind-bending to witness him switch personalities from Grizzly Adams to Dean Martin depending on the situation.

John and Nancy met, married, had five boys, and the rest is history…a very colorful history.

Everyone thinks they had an interesting childhood. At least I hope they do. I *know* I did.

This is simply a collection of stories growing up on our little farm just outside the city of Duluth, Minnesota back in the sixties. Covering my childhood from about age six to twelve years old, they are all based on true events, with a bit of fictitious embellishment where memory doesn't serve.

My purpose in writing these stories is to honor and thank my parents for everything they taught us through their example of living life to its fullest each and every day.

My goal is to tell them in a way that makes you laugh and gets you, the reader, to reflect on your childhood—your stories—the stories that made you the person you are today.

Dad always told us "life is not a dress rehearsal; you only get one chance at it—there are no do-overs."

Mom taught us how to say, *Please* and *Thank you* —and mean it.

## SWAN LAKE

When I was in elementary school we moved to the country. Our parents bought some land outside the city of Duluth, Minnesota. Swan Lake Road is over the top of the hill between the city and the airport. At the time it was a gravel road running through the heavily wooded, sparsely populated countryside of northern Minnesota. We had ten acres surrounded by literally thousands of acres of untouched forest. We practically lived in the wilderness.

There they built a brand-new house. It was a split-level ranch style nestled into a hillside. Downstairs was one bedroom, bath, recreational room (rec room), laundry room, and a garage. The upstairs had three bedrooms, one bathroom, and kitchen with open dining area family room with a big, brick corner fireplace. It was open on two sides with a large granite slab you could sit on to warm up right next to the fire. Overlooking the back yard, we had huge floor to ceiling bay windows. Heat ducts ran along the hardwood floor.

Mom placed two decorative floor pillows right in front of the bay windows. They were woven with tassels at the corners. One was turquoise blue, the other flaming orange. God-awful by today's standards, they were quite the 'in' thing at the time. Blue is my favorite color, and thus the blue pillow was unofficially mine.

While I did my fair share of playing outside, I was just as content to sit on my big blue pillow, nose plastered to the glass, and daydream. The view traveled over the backyard and into the woods. From the side bay window, I would watch the horses and cows in the pasture.

During the dead of winter, looking out over the snow-covered, frozen landscape, warm air from the heat vents enveloped me like a blanket. I would simply sit and stare out the windows, seeing everything in front of me, real and imagined. It was here that I would daydream about what was out there…in the woods…in the sky…in the world.

Thus today, when I begin to write, I mentally sit back down on my big blue pillow, look out those huge bay windows, and see the memories that make up the stories of my life.

Swan Lake Road was a state of mind as much as, if not more than, an actual place. It was our little piece of heaven on earth. This is where my stories begin.

## A SUNDAY DRIVE

Most every baby boomer can remember taking a leisurely Sunday drive with the family. Normally that meant mom and dad, brothers and sisters would hop into the car, drive to some scenic place for a picnic, and return in time to watch football (the Minnesota Vikings for everyone in Duluth) on TV. However, in the Gilbert family, the definition of a Sunday drive was anything but normal.

Typically, after the ceremonious post church "slopping of the hogs" (two hundred pancakes, three loaves of bread, two gallons of OJ, and gallon of syrup, all of which was consumed in approximately three to five minutes) everyone, all seven of us, would pile into the station wagon with all the necessary equipment.

"Equipment?" you ask.

Ah yes, the "equipment."

The minimum necessary equipment for a Gilbert Sunday drive included the following:

Food: Forty-two sandwiches, three bags of potato chips (the cheap kind), a case of generic pop (yes, it was called "pop" in Minnesota, not "soda" like the south), and one candy bar that would be cut into seven equal pieces with the sharpest, most prized jackknife in the world.

Clothes: Sixteen towels, two blankets, coats, hats, gloves (anytime in Duluth).

Other miscellaneous equipment: Three shotguns, two rifles, ammo, four fishing poles, tackle box with bobbers, oars, and of course the Grumman (canoe boat) on top.

Last, but not least, one must have one's binoculars! If by any misfortune the binoculars were left behind, no matter how far from home, the car would do an immediate one eighty when this tidbit of information became public knowledge. To retrieve the coveted ocular device was simply a matter of racing two tons of car, equipment, and family back home at speeds up to eighty miles per hour over gravel roads to get the "damn things"!

Oh yes, let's not forget our yellow lab, Bobby. Bobby usually came along for these adventures, but first he had to pass a little test. Upon noticing the car going down the driveway in an always failed attempt to sneak away without him, Bob only had to cut through the garden and successfully be clocked doing thirty before Dad would give in, stop the car, and let the slobbering, panting pile of yellow fur join the family.

Our little drives would take us to places that probably had never seen modern man. That station wagon was driven over dirt roads most people today wouldn't chance with a four-wheel drive SUV.

The most common goal of our Sunday drives was for only one purpose—to scout for ducks. Scouting for ducks is usually done by "scoping" with the "binocs."

Other activities included sighting in the rifles, shooting clay pigeons, eating, pushing the car out of a muddy rut, usually going uphill, swimming in the ice-cold water of one of Minnesota's "10,000 Lakes," watching Dad whittle a tree into a toothpick, and other fun things.

Mileage covered was from fifty to one hundred miles…one way! And crossing state lines was always a source of enjoyment. God only knows why. The day would end about seven or eight at night, when everyone had only enough energy left to unload the car, have a snack, and go to bed.

# THERE'S A PONY IN THAT CAR

One of our father's early goals was to have enough horse backs for five boys' butts. This was especially important for long rides in the country with the entire gang, including Mom and Dad. Our equine collection included three Quarter Horses, Redbird, Amber, and Stormy. Stormy was born in our garage one night during a long, loud, lightning-filled summer thunderstorm. Quarter Horses are so named because they are the fastest horse in a quarter-mile race. They obtain full speed in three strides. They are some of the calmest, safest, and most well-behaved horses in the world. The choice of ranchers for herding cattle, you would most likely see them today escorting high-strung thoroughbreds in races like the Kentucky Derby, Preakness, and

Belmont Stakes to keep them under control before loading them into the starting gates.

In addition to the Quarter Horses, we had two Welsh ponies named Bimbo and Little Red. They were smaller versions of a horse, proportional in every way. Bimbo was brown with four white stockings and what looked remarkably like the state of Minnesota painted on one side. The Welsh ponies were perfect for kids old enough to ride by themselves, yet too small to ride and control a fully-grown Quarter Horse.

Unfortunately, Dad didn't stop there. No, he thought it would be perfect to round out the collection with a Shetland pony. Shetlands are the alter ego of Quarter Horses. Stubborn as mules, they wouldn't hesitate to give you, or another horse twice their size, a good swift kick for no good reason. Maybe they suffered the horse equivalent of "short man's disease," always trying to make up for their physical stature with behavior that made them the center of attention. Originally from the Shetland Islands, these little ponies have short legs, stout, muscular bodies, and long tails that almost touch the ground. They were used to haul loaded carts out of the mines. Strong as bucking broncos, they could throw an adult rider off their little backs as if they were a ragdoll.

Fortunately for us little guys, we were still too young to ride solo on anything. Like the car, we rode in the *backseat*, which was behind the person in the saddle. This was essentially bareback riding except that we had someone to hang on to…for dear life. Walking or galloping in the backseat of a Quarter Horse was like riding in a luxury car—smooth and comfortable once you got the hang of it. The only real discomfort came in the transition to trotting. Trotting is an abrupt, jolting movement that causes the rear of the otherwise secure saddle to bounce off the horse's back. This action would create a hammer and anvil effect, which posed a significant risk of pinching the rider in the backseat. Horrifying and, frankly, traumatic for a little boy, if you get my drift!

After breakfast one quiet Sunday morning while reading the paper, Dad spotted an ad for a pony. "For Sale: One-year-old Shetland pony, white with a black head. $65.00." Well, the paper had barely hit the floor by the time the old man was calling the number in the ad.

Dad knew a good deal when he saw it, and a one-year-old pony for sixty-five dollars was a very good deal.

"Hello, I'm calling about the ad you have in today's paper for a Shetland pony. Do you still have him? You do. Can we come to see him today? We can? Great! What's your address?"

Apparently, an elderly couple in central Minnesota

had won the pony in a raffle at the local fair. He and his wife had no children and no place to keep him. In retrospect, we should have questioned his enthusiasm to meet us on such short notice…on a Sunday.

We gathered a few supplies, packed some sandwiches, and off we went for a relatively short Gilbert Sunday drive of two hours to the rural town of Princeton. The excitement was palpable. Given our *Bonanza* lifestyle, this was a big deal. We headed south on Highway 35, past Moose Lake to Hinckley, west to Milaca, through the countryside of central Minnesota to Princeton. Upon our arrival, we were greeted with the warm, friendly manner of a small town. The house had a covered porch facing a small front yard facing the street. A separate garage set back to one side created a private backyard.

"Hi, I'm John Gilbert. I called this morning about the pony you have for sale."

"Yes, sir," said the man sitting on the porch. "He's out back."

Around the side of the house, the entire Gilbert entourage followed the man. Rounding the corner between the house and garage, there he stood. Tied to a pole with a lead rope and halter was Jiggers, the Shetland pony. He had a gleaming white body, jet-black head, and the mischievous eyes of a Labrador puppy. One year old, fit and trim, Jiggers was everything we had hoped for and more. Dad didn't even try to negotiate.

"We'll take him," he said, pulling sixty-five dollars in cash out of his wallet and handing it to the owner.

"I'll get his papers for you," he said. Upon his return from the house, he handed Jiggers' papers to Dad. "When would you like to pick him up?"

"We'll take him right now," Dad said.

"Take him? How?" he asked incredulously. "You don't have a trailer!"

"Watch."

Dad took Jiggers by the lead rope and led him out from the backyard.

"Open both back doors on the car," he firmly instructed one of my older brothers. "Stand behind the open door and hold still so you don't spook him."

The rest of us stood there with the elderly couple and watched in disbelief as our father walked Jiggers from the backyard to the front, around the rear of the car, and right through the open back door.

"Shut the door when both back hooves are in the car." As the rear passenger door closed behind Jiggers, Dad stepped out the other side, turned, and shut the other door. It was one smooth operation of walking a pony up into the space between the front and back bench seats of the Ford. The man and his wife just stood there, jaws dropped, with looks of utter disbelief on their faces as the rest of us quickly jumped through the tailgate to the *way back* of the station wagon. We drove off, all seven of us, plus a pony standing in the backseat. We left the lead rope on, as that usually tricks horses and ponies into thinking they are still tied up to a hitching post, fence, or tree. Thus, there was no reason for someone to hold him and that probably would only have caused Jiggers to pull back or raise his head. No, he was simply content to stand there looking out rear window on the driver's side as we made our way back to Duluth.

We were concerned about the biggest risk we faced on our two-hour return trip to Duluth.

No, not the highway patrol pulling us over, rather we were worried about Jiggers feeling the call of nature…pony poop, to be exact. If that did happen, Dad would just turn on the car's four-by-sixty AC, by rolling down all four windows at sixty miles per hour. The potential clean up would amount to a shovel and a hose as, like most middle-class versions of a sixties station wagon, ours had that hard, impenetrable, rubberized flooring, no mats or carpet. Fortunately for us, Jiggers was so enthralled with this great adventure that he didn't realize he had to go until we got him home and safely out of the car.

The country roads were uneventful, passing through the towns that must have been the inspiration for the saying, 'It's so small, don't blink or you'll miss it.' Moreover, on a quiet Sunday afternoon, no one was out and about in these sleepy little towns. We simply made our way back to Interstate 35 North. That's where things got interesting and comical. Here we were, driving sixty miles per hour on a major highway with a pony in the back seat and, while not planned, he was looking out the driver's side of the car. Dad stayed in the slow lane as he didn't want to push it, mainly not to get pulled over for speeding and the ensuing explanation to a state trooper.

As cars passed us, people would be going about their normal Sunday Drive routines, moms and dads in the front talking about relatives, dinner, and such. Kids in back not getting along with each other, until dad uttered those infamous words, … "If I have to stop this car…!" All was normal, that is, until they passed our car that fateful day.

People in passing cars tend to glance over to inspect the passengers in the other car. Usually, this is a continuous action of heads turning, glancing, and turning back, not missing a beat in conversations, arguments, or pestering. But this Sunday, their heads stopped cold when their eyes met with a pony, looking right back at them…car to car, eye to eye. It was like freeze-framing a movie. Then, in the same instant, the passenger who made first eye contact with Jiggers slapped, hit, or squeezed any part of the person next to them to get their attention—all the while keeping their eyes locked on the pony doing sixty. The kids' reactions were the best. While their parents were engrossed in conversation or staring down the interstate, we would watch them, and upon seeing Jiggers, their eyes popped out of their heads. Not breaking eye contact, we could clearly see them shouting "THERE'S A PONY IN THAT CAR!" to which we could see the doubting parents with looks that said "sure there is, " appeasing them while thinking "what imaginations kids have"…,until of course, they made the obligatory glance over to our car. Then *their* jaws dropped, eyes popped—shocked expressions frozen as they passed.

It became a game to watch the people for their reactions to the pony in the car, which made the trip seem short. Once home, Jiggers would treat us to many wonderful years of bucking, biting, dragging little riders upside down, boots caught in stirrups on the gravel driveway, and even picking a fight with a donkey while in a living nativity one frigid Christmas Eve. But that's another story.

## LIVING NATIVITY

*A*dventure, risk taking, and sometimes "well, I thought it was a good idea at the time," was in our Gilbert DNA—especially Mom's. That trait served me well over the years, both professionally and personally. It was a simple life lesson both our parents taught us through their actions and attitude, that life is meant to be lived fully—every day. Of course, the occasional "oops" was to be expected from time to time.

Our most infamous "oops" occurred one cold Christmas Eve. We were raised in the Episcopal Church, as Mom was Lutheran and Dad, Catholic. Neither was that attached to their respective denominations, so when they were married, they flipped a spiritual coin and joined the Episcopal Church. It seemed like a nice compromise between the two, and all they really knew was they wanted church as a part of raising their family. Episcopalians serve up some mighty fine wine (usually port or brandy) for Communion. Kids couldn't wait to be confirmed so we could get a healthy snort of "the blood!" You could say the Episcopal Church had an incentive system in place for the children to attend Sunday school and Confirmation classes.

Most of the families back in the sixties had six, seven, or more kids, enough to fill an entire pew with no room to spare. With *only* five boys, JD and Nancy had a medium size brood. The Gilbert clan could spread out unless that little old couple who always arrived late were seated next to us by the usher. Then we'd shuffle sideways and sit shoulder to shoulder, butt cheek to butt cheek. This was not a good combo for five rambunctious boys. We often erupted with the picky pew persona of shoulder knocking, leg pinching, ankle kicking, and the dreaded "church" giggles during the sermon. Picky pew would simmer along until it became noticeable, whereupon we would get "the look" from Dad. That look could stop a freight train and had an equal effect on our poor church behavior. Our subsequent attention to the sermon was a get out of jail card. I thought, *if I listened to the priest I won't be in trouble when we get home*. This worked most of the time, except for the rare passing of gas echoing off the wooden pews, an untimely burp, or when some little old lady with an ill-fitting wig became the center of our attention.

Saint Paul's had a living Nativity each year for Christmas. Located next to the main entrance, it could be seen from the street for all to enjoy. It was comprised of a large wooden manger, bales of straw, and a cast of kids and animals. The cast was volunteered by over-eager parishioners, especially moms, who placed an unwarranted amount of social value and recognition on such things. The scene was completed with a large doll dressed as baby Jesus. It was simply too cold outside to have a real baby in the manger. This bitterly cold winter was the year the Gilberts were chosen for the nativity. It was an honor to be chosen, and you simply didn't pass up the opportunity due to a little cold weather. You may never get the chance again. I shudder at the thought! Thus, it began. Our contribution included my older brothers as part of the cast, bales of straw, and Jiggers, the Shetland pony. Remember what I said earlier about the "sweet" disposition of Shetlands? Jiggers was chosen due to his small size, which fit nicely into the scale of the nativity. His snow-white winter coat of hair and black head seemed like a perfect fit for the annual living Nativity right next to the huge front doors of Saint Paul's Episcopal Church —Oops.

The operational logistics of getting five boys

dressed and ready for church on a normal Sunday was a feat unto itself, let alone on a painfully cold Christmas Eve with a pony and bales of straw loaded in a horse…err…pony trailer and hitched to the station wagon. How our mother got us all suited up, into the car, and seated in a church pew without a piece of dirt, hay, straw, or anything else we could find to toss at each other was a minor miracle. She deserved a medal.

Sure, this was about attending church, but it was also about a social order, belonging, and to some extent, impressing some of the wealthiest families in Duluth. There were many, and many of them attended St Paul's. Mom grew up dirt poor, and an only child. Attending church with your kids, appropriately dressed and well-mannered, leveled the social playing field a bit. Dad didn't really care about such things, but if it was important to Nancy, then it was no big deal for him to support her. Mind you, my mother was not a shallow personality in need of external recognition. Most people we knew, rich, poor, and middle class, would have given anything to have our life on Swan Lake Road. But still, it mattered to her… at least on Sundays.

So down the driveway went the station wagon with a pony in tow. Swan Lake to Arrowhead and then down, down, down the steep hill upon which the city of Duluth was built. The church was almost at the bottom, close to Lake Superior in an affluent part of town. Once at the church, Dad parked the car on a side street running along the church grounds. My big brothers (aka the older guys) John, Jim, and Jeff, all costumed as the three Wiseman, got out of the car while Dad opened the trailer gate and unloaded Jiggers. The snow crunched under our feet. Mom and Grandma Irene, Mom's mom, hurried us little guys into the church, while the older guys assembled in front of the manger holding Jiggers in place with a lead rope. Everything would have been fine, but for the other family who was chosen to participate with us that year…along with their donkey! Mom, Grandma, my little brother Jody and I took in the spectacle for a few freezing minutes before heading inside. We were early, and as a result, got one of the coveted front pews. Mom was beaming with pride and joy as fellow parishioners made their way into the church. Adoring smiles and nods of approval for the wonderful living nativity scene, due in large part to the Gilberts, graciously floated over the pews straight to our family.

The service commenced with all the pomp and circumstance of this hallowed occasion, pews packed with us "regulars" and, of course, the seasonal Christians. Many more stood in the back and to the sides. All was good and simply perfect for Mom. However, Dad had an air of concern about him for some unknown reason. Something was amiss, and that something was about to become painfully apparent to all in attendance that fateful Christmas Eve. As the processional ended, clergy and choir assembled in their assigned seats and parishioners settled into their pews. A pastoral silence poured over the congregation like a warm blanket. The priest, standing at the pulpit, squared up the papers upon which were his notes for the sermon. Glancing down to collect his thoughts, then looking up and out over the congregation, he prepared to speak. All eyes were upon him, a warm, mindful quiet awash throughout, he opened his mouth, but all we heard was *HEEHAW…WHINNEY!*

The experienced priest started anew. Head up; look out, open mouth and once again *HEEHAW… WHINNEY*, seemed to pour out of him like bad karaoke. This time he froze with an expression of "What the hell…err…heck" (sorry, forgot where we were). Mom's face had a look of sheer horror. Mortified, staring straight forward, not moving a muscle, yet silently screaming, "Oh God, no, please, God, no!" We could tell she wanted to slink down under the pew, but she remained steadfast with proper pew posture.

Dad had a look of "crap, I knew this would happen when I saw that damn donkey!" Maybe, just maybe, this was the only outburst from the living nativity turned WWF on the front lawn of Saint Paul's Episcopal Church. The priest continued, "My friends, we are gathered here this special day to celebrate the birth of Jesus ... *HEEHAW ... WHINNEY* ... Christ."

He didn't miss a beat as a loud thud and crashing noise reverberated through the stained-glass windows. But as he continued, the pastor clearly made direct eye contact with Dad, giving him an assertive look of "please do something about this right *now*!" Dad calmly rose, turned, and walked down that excruciatingly long aisle to the main entrance of the church. He must have been fuming, "We couldn't sit in the *rear* of the church—No, that wasn't good enough for such an occasion!" All the parishioners did their best to look forward and not make eye contact with JD, but the attention was squarely on him and the breakdown of peace on earth outside. It was not on the pastor giving the most important sermon of the year. I'm certain, were it not for the time and place, everyone would have been right behind him, heading out the front doors to see the big fight.

Right as he opened the enormous, wooden front door, which only served to amplify the audible action, one of my brothers shouted, "JIGGERS...KNOCK IT THE HELL OFF!" This unintended message of the Christmas spirit shot through the open door, echoed off the cavernous stone walls of the Cathedral, and hit the pastor's ears like a shotgun blast. Even with the door finally closed, we could still hear Dad shout, "Crap, get that damn donkey out of here now!"

Upon reaching the scene of the crime, it was clear Jiggers was not in the Christmas spirit. He'd attacked the donkey, biting, kicking and generally objecting to the presence of this inferior creature. One of Jigger's attempts to kick the donkey missed the mark and hit the wooden manger, breaking it into kindling wood and knocking baby Jesus across the front lawn and headfirst into a snowbank. Dad stopped in his tracks for the briefest of seconds. There, before his anguished eyes, was a knocked down nativity, splintered manger, straw strewn everywhere, baby Jesus half-buried with only his little bare feet sticking out of the snow. Mary was in tears, Joseph was in shock, and Jiggers and the donkey were still going at each other, kicking, biting, whinnying and heehawing.

Dad took control of the situation, grabbing Jiggers by the halter with such strength and authority the little Shetland knew he was in deep doo-doo. He led him directly back to the trailer while barking out orders to the boys to chase down the donkey, lift the nativity, pull baby Jesus out of the snowbank, and try to reassemble the splintered wood into something that passed for a manger.

Once the snow settled and cast members were back in character, Dad had the donkey tethered by the two oldest boys. With Jiggers safely locked up in pony jail, Dad made his way back into the church. Straightening his jacket and tie, he calmly proceeded back up the aisle to the front pew, he turned and sat down in his place as the priest finished the sermon. Almost on cue, the choir broke into an enthusiastic, if not celebratory, rendition of *Joy to the World*.

I could see a reassuring glance from the priest to Dad that clearly said, "Thank you!"

The service proceeded on with all its grand Christmas traditions. And while it wasn't the way Mom had pictured it, we had yet another Gilbert story to laugh about in the years to come.

# ANIMAL FARM

Animals, animals, everywhere we had animals. Horses, cows, ducks, geese, pheasants, quail, and chickens, we had all shapes and sizes. They were bought, bred, born or hatched, then raised to adulthood. Some were for pleasure and show, some butchered for food, and some released into the wild to regenerate the population.

One thing they all had in common was poop, piles, and piles of poop. Horses pooped piles of tennis ball size turds. Cows, on the other hand, dropped wet, steaming patties in one large, thick pie while never missing a beat from their grazing. It was like nothing at all happened with the only discernable action of raising their tails up to avoid contact with the effluent. I say "attempt" as this was usually not too successful. One only had to view the backside of a cow to see they are not very adept at avoiding themselves while…um…voiding themselves.

By the way, milk cows (dairy), have their teats—yes, that's what they're called, city folk—located directly below all this dang dung. Think about that the next time you pour pretty, pasteurized milk all over your Post Toasties!

Now it was easy to avoid the fresh cow patties as they were shining, steaming, stinking platters of poop. However, beware the cool-n-crusties! Cool-n-crusties appeared on the outside to be old, dried patties. We couldn't resist tossing them at each other like thick, green, organic Frisbees. Cool-n-crusties were akin to undercooked pancakes, done on the outside, but raw and gooey inside. Step on one and your foot would break through the crust into still liquid poop on the inside. The goo would ooze up in between your toes and stick there like thick pudding. They would implode if you attempted to pick one up and fling it at someone and it would implode all over you with the intended targets of your attack, laughing hysterically—at least until they stepped on one. Still, that didn't stop us boys from trying.

Running away from a tormenting sibling in hot pursuit with a properly cured patty intended for your head wasn't safe either. If you were lucky, you stomped straight down on it and just kept on running. However, if you hit a patty on the heel of your foot, you were doomed to slip and fall on your butt, sliding right through it, leaving a green streak of cow poop running up your back. Then, to add insult to injury, you would be caught and hit with an old pie by the one who "Started it, Mom!"

During the summer all these nature calls were spread out over acres of pasture like a minefield. Many animals equal many mines. It was a different matter altogether during the frigid winter months. Like all proper farms, we had a barn. Ours was not big, red, and round at the top, but rather a modern, more inexpensive model. It was rectangular with an angled roof and two large sliding doors. The inside was divided in half by a heavily built wood fence with a gate to pass from one side to the other. One side was for storing hay. The other provided shelter for the horses and cows. They would spend most of the cold winter days huddled inside the barn. The only warmth provided was their thick winter coats of hair. To help, we had horse blankets which ran from neck to tail and loosely strapped underneath their bellies like saddles. The cows weren't as fortunate.

Well now, envision a half dozen horses and several cows all huddled together on their side of the barn eating, drinking, and you guessed it…pooping for the entire winter. No, they did not go outside in the forty below temps to relieve themselves as a courtesy to their fellow barn mates. It was a continuous cycle of food in one end and out the other…all winter long. Come springtime, the roof of the barn was noticeably lower on the inside. This was due to the winter long poop fest raising the level of the floor. There were layers upon layers of hoof-packed, frozen dung.

This, of course, resulted in one of our many annual traditions—the spring cleaning of the barn floor. With the herd out in the pasture once again, our job was to clean out the poop layer cake. You would think the simple solution would be to let it completely thaw out top to bottom. But this option would lead to one huge, sloppy mess that would run off shovels and wheelbarrows, making the task considerably more difficult and time-consuming. Think green, frozen smoothie.

No, the best way to remove frozen animal dung is to let it thaw enough to get a shovel in and under several inches, push forward with your boot, then press down on the handle, causing a good size chunk to break off in a still hardened state. These flat chunks were easier to shovel into the wheelbarrow leaving the next frozen layer exposed to the warm spring air to thaw. Repeating the same process, it took days to get down to the dirt floor.

The resulting mountain of crap would eventually be sold to neighbors as composted fertilizer for their gardens. Only JD could sell shit!

If someone were to ask me what my dad did, I could honestly say he sold shit. They would ask "What sort of shit?"

I would reply "No…shit…he sells shit."

"No shit?" they would reply in surprised disbelief.

"No, shit."

## TED THE ATTACK CHICKEN

Blazing orange feathers, huge blood-red comb atop his head, and a tail that would make a peacock jealous, he proudly stood guard over the backyard. A fancy chicken historically bred for fighting, but now for show at the local 4-H county fair, his name was Ted.

This was not your plain old farm chicken, fat, dumb, and lazy. No, this was a fighting cock with the disposition of his DNA to prove it. He was beautiful, especially in the early morning light. The rising sun would turn on his luminescent feathers like a neon sign. In addition to his amazing colors, Ted sported long, needle-like spurs, one on the back of each leg. In the wild, they would be used to fend off predators and fight other males for the right to mate with their harem of hens.

Facing each other, neck low to the ground, heads dancing back and forth, eyes locked onto their foe, two males would perform a ritual pre-fight, circular dance. Then, suddenly and simultaneously, the two run at each other, leaping straight up into the air just before impact. Using their wings to steady themselves and maneuver, they kick their legs out and thrust those long spurs toward their opponent, attempting to, and often succeeding in, killing the loser.

Ted usually wasn't aggressive toward us...with one exception. Like most kids, our inventory of toys included a basketball. Basketballs are orange like you know who. Of course, we always left the ball out in the backyard when called in to wash up for dinner. At some point on his daily rounds of the Kingdom of Ted, he encountered Ms. Wilson. It must have looked like a big, plump hen to him. Ted was in love! Strutting around the basketball, extending his wings, tail feathers straight up in a "look at how big mine is" mode, he would make a low mating call of... bwaaaak...bwaaaak.

Then, when the moment was right and *she* appeared ready, Ted would jump on top of the basketball, and while flapping his wings for balance, he would...uh...well...he would start humping Ms. Wilson right there in the backyard. With all the energy and spirit of a fighting cock, he would go at her like there was no tomorrow. Ted could have written the Kama Sutra for Chickens as he did things to that basketball that defied gravity and showed creative genius. When done consummating the marriage, he would fall off, exhausted, and proudly walk under a shade tree for a well-deserved nap.

Naturally, we would watch these romantic interludes from the big picture windows overlooking the backyard, the older guys providing real-time, adolescent commentary while us little guys naively giggled. We thought it looked funny.

Combine Ted's fighting DNA with his passion to protect the love of his life and no one dared get too close to the basketball. Anyone stupid enough to approach it would be subjected to the wrath of Ted. The other chickens, ducks, geese, dogs, and even an errant pony were in danger. Get too close to the basketball and all you would see is a blur of orange streaking right at you. Head down, wings extended, yellow legs running like mad…you were dead 'Ted' meat!

Running away was futile. Your only hope was to limit the impending wounds to something less than an arterial bleed. With flapping wings, he would leap off the ground and hammer you with those razor-sharp spurs, impaling your legs and thighs, leaving multiple, needle-like holes bleeding from your flesh. Ted the Attack Chicken was going to kill you or at least make you think twice before threatening Ms. Wilson ever again.

The basketball remained in the same spot all summer long. In fact, we didn't pick it up until the first snow covered *her* in a white blanket, camouflaging the orange hen from Ted's lustful eyes.

Ted's passion for that ball would be his ultimate demise. Blinded by love, he would stay out in the middle of the yard, guarding his love when predators approached, and all other fowl retreated to the protection of their respective coops. One romantic fall day a huge hawk swooped down and picked Ted right off the basketball while in a fit passion with the Mrs. Up, up, and away the bird of prey flew, Ted firmly grasped by its powerful talons. In a flash of orange feathers, Ted was gone.

We left the basketball in that place as a memorial to him. In time it deflated, like having an emotional letdown. Ms. Wilson looked sad and depressed.

Alas, we never replaced him. There could only ever be one Ted the Attack Chicken.

## CHICKEN PLUCKING

They say necessity is the mother of invention. When you have horses and cows you need to feed them…a lot…every day. This was even more important in Duluth, as the long harsh winters covered the pastures with several feet of snow. With nothing to graze on, the animals were dependent on us to feed them until the grass reappeared in the spring. We needed extra money to help pay for a barn load of hay to feed the horses and cows through the winter. Most kids mowed lawns or had paper routes to make a buck, but we weren't 'most' kids. Further, living in the country where your neighbors live a mile apart and well off the road didn't lend itself to having a paper route. The solution —a chicken route, of course. Isn't it obvious? We had the resources of land and labor, and Dad provided the know-how. How he obtained all this know-how, I'll never know. He grew up in the city as the son of a banker, for crying out loud, and Future Farmers of America usually come from…well…farms.

Phase one required two things—baby 1) chickens or pullets, and 2) a place to grow them, which was a brooder. A brooder looks like a small oven on wheels with several shelves or levels made of wire mesh. It provided the same protective warmth of a mother hen. The shelves were small enough for the chicks to stand on without their tiny, clawed feet falling through and getting caught, but large enough to allow, you guessed it, their poop to drop through and onto a tray below. We lovingly referred to these as "cookie trays." Lined with newspaper, the "cookies" had to be removed daily. This was done by simply pulling the tray out and rolling soiled newspaper into a large, poop-filled Stromboli. The 'Stromboli' was carefully placed in a wheelbarrow which would then be dumped on Mt. Manure for composting. I say "carefully," as chickens don't have separate anatomy for pee. It all comes out in a squirt so to speak. If the term "shart" means anything, you get the picture. Thus a 'Shartboli' was soft, weak, and wet. Hold too tight and your fingers would tear through, and no, we didn't wear gloves! Don't support it correctly and it would break in half all over the floor. Now this didn't bother us in the least, so we didn't "toss our cookies," but boys will be boys, so a little cookie tossing at each other usually made it into the mix.

By now you might be thinking I have some sort of fixation with poop, but unless you have lived on a farm, you simply have no idea how much crap all these animals produced each and every day. And it all had to be managed. Before getting an MBA, I had earned my MMA—Masters of Manure Administration! But I digress.

The brooder phase was only several weeks long, as chickens grow fast. Eventually, they would be relocated to the small barn in phase two.

Like its bigger brother, the small barn was divided into two equal parts. In this case, it was two rooms with a connecting door. The front part was for all the farm tools (shovels, pitchforks, saws, a post hole digger, loppers, etc.) and horse tack (saddles, bridles, leads, brushes and hoof picks, etc.) and feed. The back room was for the chickens in the spring and summer and the ducks and geese in the winter. It had a small opening like a dog door with a ramp that allowed them to go outside to a fenced pen during the day. In the evening we would herd them all back up the ramp into the barn and secure the door to protect them from predators like fox, mink, and owls. We were literally preventing the fox from getting into the hen house.

Eventually, after a couple of months, the chickens

were fully grown, plump, and ready for plucking. "How many chickens?" you ask—two hundred. It would take several weekends to get through the entire clutch, as the last step in the process is very time-consuming. Phase three began with Dad rising early to get the fire started. Behind the house, the land dropped off to a low area in the woods. The hill was steep enough for some good sledding in the winter, as long as you avoided the trees. At the bottom, there was a clearing with a large fire pit right in the middle. Once he had a roaring fire of birch wood logs going, it was time to roust everyone from bed. Oh, yeah, even our widowed grandmother Irene and Mom were part of the labor force for this big event.

Both washtubs in the basement were filled with the ice-cold water piped in directly from Lake Superior. A hose was run from the house down to the clearing was used to fill a large, galvanized tub which would be placed on a steel grate directly over the fire. The water was heated just short of boiling. Near the back of the clearing was a long, smallish diameter pole made from a poplar tree, all branches removed and attached horizontally with a rope between two large trees about head high. Along the pole, there were nooses made of twine placed about two feet apart along its entire length.

Now it was time. Dad and the older guys would go up to the chicken coop, grab two chickens each, and carry them by the legs, upside down, wings a-flappin' and cackling like they were about to meet their maker…which they were. Who says chickens are stupid?

Out of the coop, across the backyard, and down the hill they would go. Once there, Dad would hang them upside down by the feet, where they would continue their protests and wing flappin'. It took several trips to get the entire pole filled.

Dad would take out the sharpest jackknife in the world and beginning at one end of the line of upside-down chickens, he would slit their jugulars right in the neck. They would bleed out, and by the time he got to the end of the line, the first half were…um… kosher. Lifting and loosening the leg nooses, everyone was handed a dead chicken. Forming a circle around the tub of steaming hot water over the fire pit, Dad would grab a chicken by the feet, and dunk it in the scalding hot water. Then, he would push it under with a stick to make sure the entire bird had been completely submerged a couple of times, before handing it to the plucker. This process allowed you to simply grab a handful of feathers and in one controlled downward motion, roll them right off the body. Once plucked, the bird was taken up to the house and placed in the washtubs of ice water for holding until the entire batch for the day had been plucked—usually forty to fifty chickens.

We had this down to a science. As the initial line was being plucked, someone would go back to the coop and begin restocking the pole. At some point in the morning, it was a continuous process of hauling, hanging, plunging, and plucking.

The end of this phase left a scene akin to some sort of ancient sacrificial ceremony. Stepping back, you would overlook a steaming cauldron of hot, feather-filled water. The circle around the fire pit was blanketed in a thick, wet carpet of white feathers. Pan a little up, and there in the back stood the hanging post with a line of fresh blood pooling along the entire length, slowly seeping into the ground beneath. Cold, damp, enshrouded by the trees with steam rising from the still-hot tub of water over the now smoldering fire, it was right out of a medieval movie scene like *Braveheart* after a battle. But the sight never lingered or disturbed. We had work to do…. much more work.

All hands moved up to the garage, where folding tables were arranged for the next production line. The first step was to retrieve enough chilled birds from the ice-cold waterfilled tubs for each plucker to become a gutter. Dad would cut the heads and lower yellow legs off, dumping them into a five-gallon plastic bucket. Then he would use that same jackknife to slice open the cavity near the back, bottom of the bird. Most people would recognize this as the place where they put stuffing. Then he would pass it down the line for gutting. Somewhat akin to cleaning out a pumpkin before carving it into a Jack O'Lantern, you 'simply' insert your entire hand into this opening with outstretched fingers and follow the cavity walls of the chicken's insides. Once your hand reaches the end near the neck, you grab and pull. This motion, done correctly, would result in nearly all the innards coming out in one, gooey, handful of chicken guts. That one motion continues out and over the side of the table, dropping the mess into a bucket.

It was critical to not break the small green sack that held the digested food before it was eliminated. Break the green sack while inside the cavity and the bird would be contaminated, ruined, and could not be sold for human consumption. At least the dogs were happy with the eventual, boiled chicken feast. But Dad would be pissed, and you did not want to be at the receiving end when he found out you destroyed a bird and its profits, due to inattention. Reenter the cavity maybe a couple more times to remove any bits left behind and pass it down the line to the person in charge of pulling any remaining feather quills that held on from the initial plucking. This was done using a pair of pliers or tweezers, depending on the size and location of the quills.

The final step in the cleaning phase was to burn off what looked like frizzy hair with a candle. Hold the now bare and hollow chicken over a large candle, taking care not to burn the skin, rotate with two hands, and let the tip of the candle singe off any unsightly, remaining 'frizzy' stuff.

By this time, the former flapping, feathered fowl now looked like what you see in the grocery store. The roaster would be placed back in one of the washtubs refilled with fresh, ice-cold water for holding until the final phase, which included bagging, weighing, pricing, and finally delivering to customers (neighbors) who had preordered our somewhat famous and very desirable homegrown roasting chickens. The entire process from peeping baby chicks to roaster delivery ran from spring, over the summer, and ended about the time farmers were harvesting and baling their crops. Plucking done, roasters delivered, and money collected, it was time for us to order a truckload of hay for the impending winter.

# GIRLS AND HAY BALES

Scouring the Sunday classifieds at the end of the short Minnesota summer, we would find "hay for sale" ads. It was important to look for alfalfa. While the price range could be from 50 – 75 cents per bale, it was well worth it to pay a bit more to get a high content of alfalfa, as it provided more nutritional value to the horses and cows. Better hay reduced our overall feed cost. Without it, we would have to buy many more sacks of expensive grain mixed with molasses to sustain the animals throughout the harsh winter. Think of grain as steak, and alfalfa as the veggies.

After a few phone calls to different farmers, Dad would place the order for several hundred bales. On delivery day, everyone was home waiting for the huge flatbed truck. We would hear it first, laboring through its gears to haul the heavy load of hay down Swan Lake Road. Slowing to a complete stop; we could see they were verifying the address on our mailbox before making the turn onto our long gravel driveway. The old flatbed truck was stacked so high with bales, it looked like it was about to topple over at any second.

Dad directed the driver around the little barn and through the big gate into the upper pasture where the big barn was located. Meanwhile, the rest of the gang would jump into action. That is, the older guys would be out next to the big barn ready to unload the truck. Us little guys were ordered to stay out of the way. We were too small to help. Jody, the youngest of the bunch, was content to stay in the house and watch with Mom from the big picture window facing the upper pasture and barns. I would go outside but stayed back a good distance from moving trucks and falling hay bales.

All the horses and cows had been moved to the lower pasture, which was fenced and gated off, to keep them out of the way. Unloading a truckload of hay was hard enough on its own. We didn't need thousands of pounds of hooved eating machines getting in the way.

Once the truck was parked and everyone was in place, it was time to begin the unloading process. The farmer brought help as well, usually his sons, and in this case, his daughter joined the team. In the words of Thumper, from the movie *Bambi*, I was "twitterpated!" She was a goddess sent to me from the hayfields of southern Minnesota. As I watched from afar, the operation began with the farmer climbing atop the Leaning Tower of Pisa, while his sons untied the ropes holding the load together and secured to the flatbed. There was a method to tossing bales of hay from atop the pile so they would land on the bound sides and not break apart upon impact with the ground. If they broke, we couldn't haul and stack them into the barn.

When the first bale hit the ground, the first one in line would pick it up by the bailing twine and carry it into the barn. Dad and my big brothers, along with the farmers' kids, including his daughter, would grab two bales, one in each hand, and briskly haul them into the barn. The farmer would drop the bales in a line from the back to the front of the truck and then repeat, layer after layer. This would allow him to continue dropping bales from on high without hitting anyone. But with many hands working efficiently, the bales seemed to be dropping ahead of the next person in line.

Inside the big barn, the entire process was essentially reversed. Beginning at the back of the barn, the bales would be stacked like Legos, up and out. Row by row, layer by layer, the entire load of hay was transferred from truck to barn in one continuous process of dropping, hauling, and stacking until the truck was bare and the barn was full.

Normally it was all well and good for me to simply watch the event. But this year was different. I was just old enough to know that girls existed, and they were special for some reason, but too young to know how or why. My eyes were fixated on the farmer's daughter. Watching her every move, her long, flowing, blond hair waving back and forth was mesmerizing. I'm certain we made eye contact; certain she looked right at me. I watched in amazement and awe as she stepped right up, grabbed two bales of hay, and effortlessly hauled them into the barn.

Well, not to be shown up by a girl, and to impress her, I stepped right up too (for the first time in my life) and grabbed two bales. This was not a good idea. Instead of me grabbing the bales, the bales grabbed me. I was stopped dead in my tracks, hands caught in the baling twine, anchored to the ground; my feet flew right out from under me. Falling flat on my face, I couldn't move, couldn't escape, couldn't hide, and couldn't get out of the way of the next hay bomb. I had only seconds to move as the delivery process stopped for no one—not even a lovestruck kid lying on the ground between two bales like some sort of country crucifix. The farmer's daughter hadn't come out of the barn yet. Mortified, the thought of getting crushed by a flying bale of hay was better than her seeing me in this predicament. Frantically, I extricated myself and stood up when the hay goddess reappeared on her way back for another TWO bales! As she approached, I thought that hauling one bale was better than none. It would at least explain why I was standing in the line right next to the truck. Surely, I would be able to man…err…boy handle ONE bale.

Wrong! The best I could muster was to drag the damn thing from truck to barn, leaving an oh so obvious trail carved into the dirt that led straight to me. I could only hope the Nordic goddess wouldn't notice. But of course, as we passed going opposite directions, she turned her head and looked at me with a smirk of pleasure, if not a bit of empathy for the little boy trying to impress her. She even lapped me on her return trip. God, how I wanted to be buried alive behind the ever-growing stack of hay!

Upon reflection, this was probably the moment that determined I was destined for management.

## THE HAY BOX HORROR

*I*f you were thinking there can't possibly be anything more to say about hay, you're wrong. I have one more little yarn to spin. You see, all that hay we stacked up in the barn was there for only one reason…to feed hungry horses and cows, a.k.a. large, heavy, hooved beasts with attitudes, especially around dinner time. We had a hay box into which a couple of bales would be tossed, twine pulled off, and the hay spread about the bottom so all bovine and equine diners could gather around the perimeter to eat. Of course, we couldn't have some regular old box bought from the local farm and feed store. No, they weren't big enough or built strong enough to handle the Gilbert herd. Funny, this was back in the sixties when things were made "the way they used to make them." Horses and cows have a nasty habit of gnawing on anything and everything, especially wood. Fence posts, trees, even the corners of the barn bore signs of what appeared to be giant beavers.

The hay box had to stand up to these constant attacks, in addition to a ton of living rump roast using the box to scratch an itch in those hard to get to places. Thus, Dad made his own hay box on steroids. Constructed of 4" X 6" lumber, it measured 8' X 12' and stood 4' high. The bottom was covered with ¾" plywood making it so heavy that not even full-grown horses and cows could push it around. But the mere size and weight did nothing to prevent their urge to gnaw along the edges. To slow the gnawing and extend the usable life of the hay box, we would apply and reapply multiple coats of creosote. I don't how this stuff was made, but it was generally used on telephone/power poles to prevent against rotting and termites. An industrial-grade, thick, black goo that smelled like turpentine, it was effective at keeping the herd at bay.

The nightly feeding was usually no big deal for my older brothers. As teenagers living on a farm, they had the strength and skill to yank a couple of bales from the stack, haul them out to the box imitating a battleship, toss, spread, and leave before the animals figured it out and began their mad dash from the pasture upon realizing there was fresh hay to eat. However, as time passed, my older brothers were frequently gone. Whether due to enlisting in the Navy, busy with high school, part-time jobs at the grocery store, or in one case, developing talent for delegation, I found myself saddled (pun intended) with the chore.

Recalling my bale handling prowess, it became abundantly clear this was a disaster in the making. Timing was critical to my survival. I would spy out from the picture window in the living room. It provided a pretty good view of the upper pasture and the big barn. The pasture fell off down a hill, so the herd could be just over the crest, or hopefully, grazing way out in the lower pasture. The lower pasture required the herd to pass through an open gate located at the end of the fence line that bisected the two fields. The trip from lower to upper, and eventually the hay box next to the barn, would give me ample time to load the box with hay and get out of harm's way. If they were hanging around the barn, I was toast. Regardless, it always became a race between the herd and me.

Unfortunately, the chore gods were often against me. Upon my initial surveillance from the safety of the house, it appeared the herd was at least over the hill and not loitering around the barn. I needed to sneak out to the barn without drawing the attention of my hooved friends. Exiting the house from the garage, I kept the barn between myself and the pasture to not been seen. Once in the pasture, I'd hug the side of the barn, and slowly, quietly peer around the corner like a farm boy version of Inspector Clouseau. Usually, I was successful in getting around and into the barn without detection. Once there, I had to grab and drag the first bale out to the hay box, lift, shove, drop it to the bottom, and head back to the barn as fast as I could for the second bale. You see, while horses and cows don't have great eyesight, nature gave them great big ears for defense against predators. They were ultra-sensitive, and when it came to food, they worked like radar or in this case 'Haydar.' I could see all the ears pop straight up in unison when the first bale hit the bottom of the box. The race was on! As I ran back to the barn for the second bale, I could hear them running up the hill. It sounded like rolling thunder, but the situation wasn't dire until I could feel the ground shake from the pounding hooves. That happened about the time I was dragging the last bale with all my might out of the barn door. The distance between barn and box felt like it was getting longer the closer they got. Heart pounding, ground rumbling, bale dragging behind me like a lead anchor—enter religion. *Oh please, God, let me get to the box, I don't want to be trampled to death!*

I hit the box at full speed, heaved the bale over the side, and jumped in right on top. Landing with a thud,

I started coughing out hay impaled into my mouth while scrambling to the center of the box. Seconds later the herd jolted to a stop and began fighting each other for a place around the Hay Box from Hell. Snorting, kicking, and even biting was augmented with flying saliva (think big Pavlov's dogs) and farting.

I sat on the bottom of a giant wooden box, living my own version of Orwell's *Animal Farm*, trying not to get eaten alive and wondering if anyone would even notice if I did. Eventually, the jockeying for position was sorted out, the biting and kicking transitioned into a harmonious choir of munching. *Munch, munch, crunch, crunch*. I located the widest opening between two of my hooved friends, jumped out, ran around the barn, ducked under the fence, and back to the safety of our house.

*God, I hope they're in the lower pasture tomorrow*!

## BURNED APPLES

Living in the country was a great place for five boys. It was, quite frankly, a wise, if not brilliant, decision by our parents to provide the best possible environment to raise a family—especially boys. At a minimum, the worst trouble we could find was a mud-fest around the duck ponds or tossing dried cow patties at each other in the pasture…although arming us with pitchforks and shovels to clean the barn probably wasn't the brightest of ideas. Most of the time the daily chores were enough to keep us occupied, but every so often someone would get it in their head to try something new. Usually that "someone" was our mother, and probably because she thought we had picked up enough rocks, the lawn was mowed, and Dad wasn't home clearing brush with his infamous loppers. Or she sensed an impending implosion if the troops weren't kept occupied. But mostly, she loved getting us all together for some event like a picnic or party. She always wanted everyone to be happy…at the same time…together…all five boys! Why do moms try to make siblings get along instead of doing something simple, like say, world peace?

One summer day, there was only *one* summer day in Duluth, Mom decided we should all go for a horseback ride and picnic. We had just enough horse backs to carry every soon-to-be sore butt in the family. I, being one of "the little guys," would always ride…err…bounce behind someone. Thank God, as Jiggers would have been the likely starter pony. If he could, he would have painted little riders on his neck like aces, for every time he threw one of us off his little Shetland back, like fighter pilots did in WWII.

Usually these were spur-of-the-moment events, followed by packing enough food for the animals, and I don't mean the horses. While Mom was getting the food ready, the older guys would begin the saddling process. Of course, one had to collect a horse to saddle it, which was usually accomplished with a bribe consisting of a handful of sweet oats followed by haltering and attaching a lead rope. Upon tying to the hitching post, their hooves had to be inspected, and if necessary, remove anything that could hurt them during the ride. This was accomplished with a hoof pick. While gently pushing one leg forward behind the knee, the horse would comply by settling his weight on the other three legs and allow you to pull the hoof backward and up to inspect and clean. Remember those cow patties? At one point they were fresh and hot. Now it was impacted poop. Once the hooves were clean, the horses were saddled and bridled.

The rider would mount up and pull passengers like me and Jody up and behind. Then down the gravel driveway, right on to Swan Lake Road, and off to some open country fields. Early on in this single line processional one of the horses would relieve themselves. Usually, the lead horse would lift its tail and take a walking crap, a steaming, horrid smelling crap.

Well, if you think the power of suggestion applies only to humans, you are wrong. The lead horse would cause a chain reaction from the front of the line to the back, and since I was on the back of the horse in the back of the line, that meant an excruciatingly long period of clip clopping through crap. What a joyful experience!

Now no good ride happens without traveling over some of northern Minnesota's hilly landscape. If there was a direct, flat, and open route, or a narrow, mosquito-infested, tree branch attacking path traversing rocks, gullies, and occasional water of some kind, there wasn't even a question. We always took the Alaskan Yukon route. If the horses didn't work up a good sweat and someone didn't almost fall off, it simply wasn't authentic. Having your stomach acid churned by the prospect of impending bodily harm was a prerequisite to a successful ride. At least this was my perspective on the matter.

On one of these outings, Mom decided to add a new twist to the mid-ride picnic…apples cooked over an open campfire. Something she probably read in *Good Housekeeping*. I can only imagine! Well, the first problem with this picture is Mom is a Finlander—people not known for their culinary prowess. The Finns make English cooking look like French cuisine. Now, try to take that background and apply it to a recipe from a ladies' magazine, and try to pull it off during a horseback ride in the woods.

Upon arriving at or, better said, stopping due to hunger pains in a randomly stumbled-upon clearing, the *Bonanza* crew would dismount, or, in my case, fall, off the beasts and tie them to a nearby tree. If it was a hot day, like over sixty degrees in Duluth, we would take the saddles and blankets off to let them cool. Then we made a fire, ate everything preassembled, and waited with dog-drooling anticipation Mom's new treat. She drenched apples in some sort of brown sugar-n-syrup concoction, wrapped them in aluminum foil, and placed them around the open fire. It seemed like an eternity waiting for them to be pronounced done, especially once the flies found out there were horses and food in the neighborhood. At least the horses had tails to swat away the damn things. Flies, by the way, were an inconvenience. Horseflies, on the other hand, could inflict bodily harm and leave open wounds with a single bite. Did I mention this was a happy childhood memory?

Well, after much anticipation, the moment finally arrived. It was time to unwrap the *pièce de résistance*. This first of firsts, this new and creative masterpiece as only Mom could make. We all stood around the still-crackling fire as the sugar-coated baked apples were lovingly removed and handed out, one for each of us. The first impression was that of scalding hot syrup causing second degree burns on the tongues of our over-eager palates. Of course, we all kept trying to eat them. This was followed by the virtually simultaneous chewing and tasting of *burned* apples… crisp and black on the outside, raw on the inside.

Understand, it wasn't easy to disappoint this crew when it came to food, but the immediate and unanimous facial expressions were ones of horror. Horror from the bitter, burnt taste swirling in our mouths collided with the horror of whether we should spit or swallow. We were caught in the excruciating dilemma of either hurting Mom's feelings or ingesting this science experiment gone bad. We all tried to swallow, but the nonverbal assessment was one of pure disgust.

Thank God Mom saved our little behinds by swiftly and emphatically announcing her own proclamation of, "Oh these are just awful!" and with her own elimination of the concoction from her mouth, freed us to do the same. We all followed with a group spitting of the apples upon the pristine Minnesota countryside, followed by uproarious laughter led by none other than Mom. We doused the fire, saddled up, and rode home with yet another fond Gilbert memory.

# THE TALK

The Duluth Public Schools were progressive for the sixties, especially for the Midwest. One specific area of pushing the social norms envelope was sex education. In the sixth grade, before we were sent off to middle school and the advent of raging hormones, the school system waded into the parental waters of "the talk." I'm betting most parents were fine with this, even a bit relieved. The girls and boys were separated, with the female teachers assigned to the girls, and the male teachers to the boys. There were diagrams of both male and female anatomies. The lesson was complete, thorough and very descriptive on the matter of fluid mechanics —so to speak. Most of the class sat in stunned silence, permeated with a few scattered, nervous giggles.

I was interested in the human aspect of where babies came from, but not shocked in the least by most of what was presented that day. Growing up on a farm, we had witnessed all forms of God's creatures yielding to the annual urges of mating season. During springtime, there was lovemaking happening all over the place. Morning, noon, and night, chickens, ducks, quail, and pheasants were humping each other...amongst their own kind of course.

Sometimes we would laugh at the sight and sounds of God's little creatures making more little creatures, but most of the time, we would go about our chores and the animals went about theirs as we walked right by them. The game birds, waterfowl, and chickens looked like a mass of flying feathers all around the yard and in their pens. The ducks and geese would do it on land or at sea. Splashing away with their wings to stay atop the water, it was a wonder they both didn't drown.

Fast and furious, the animal acts of love were usually over in a couple of minutes. But with all the feathers, we couldn't really see what was happening between the two. And with the outcome being a bunch of eggs in a nest, not an actual chick or duckling, the story of the birds and the bees remained a mystery.

We also bred our dogs and sold the puppies, but that 'process' only provided an image of two dogs locked together with Dad holding them in place until the male dog could be separated from the female. They were literally locked together and all we were told was the male dog could be hurt if he tried to get away after he was done. *But done with what?* We didn't have a clear picture of why or what this meant.

We found out when Dolly, our Springer Spaniel, started having puppies a few months later. Now, this left no questions as to where puppies came from and how they got out of her belly. Still, questions remained about how they got there in the first place. Additionally, that memory took a backseat to what happened leading up to her giving birth. We had let her out to go to pee, or so we thought. There was still snow on the ground, and when she squatted, she gave birth to the first puppy right on top of a snowbank. Dolly looked back at the squirming little mass in a sack, turned away, and ran right back into the house. It was as if she said to herself, *What the hell is that and where did it come from!* We rescued the snow pup, and Dolly figured out her maternal role in the course of delivering eleven more puppies that evening. By this time any sex education value was gone in an instant.

The real show, however, was when we were breeding Quarter Horses. We had the mares, Big Red and Amber. Dad would arrange for a stud to be brought out to the farm. Yes, there was a stud fee. Man, what a way to make a living!

When the time had arrived, he would make the call and the stud's owner would trailer him out to meet the lucky lady. Only Dad, my older brothers, and the stud's owner were allowed in the pasture. Jody and I were banned to the safety of the house. These are big animals, and studs by nature are very aggressive. This was not a task for the faint of heart and you had to be able to move fast to get out of the way.

They would hold the mare in place with a lead rope while the stud sniffed around her. At first, she would try to run away, kicking and bucking. The courtship would go on for a while until *she* was ready. Then the stud would rear up on his hind legs and mount her from behind. While an incredible act to watch, you still had to pay attention as the whole act only lasts about a minute. But oh, what a hot minute!

I didn't need binoculars to see *EVERYTHING* from the living room window. We were almost a football field away from the action, but I can assure you there were NO questions about what *it* was for, and how *it* worked. I thought, "Oh my god, look at the size of that thing!" That "thing" was almost a couple feet long with proportional girth to boot. It practically hit the ground once he finished and was standing on all fours again.

Shocked, I finally understood the birds and the bees. There was no need for "the talk." Worse, I felt inadequate in that department for many years to come. After seeing a horse's *thing* at full attention, you can't measure up…ever…for the rest of your life!

The connection between that special health class at Birchwood Elementary School and the breeding of horses all rudely came together one night after we were put to bed. A couple of us shared the bedroom right across the hallway from our parents. Often, we would hear their bed squeaking, which led to uncontrollable giggling, which in turn lead to a stern command emanating through the closed doors from Dad to "Go to sleep!" The squeaking would stop for a bit and then resume, instigating another round of giggles.

But one squeaking night, as I was about to burst into laughter, the school health class, horse breeding, and bed squeaking all collided in my brain. It was like a horrific cosmic bomb exploding inside me with the realization of what Mom and Dad were up to across the hall. They were "doing it!"

Do you remember the first time you realized your parents had sex? I mean to the burning, agonizing core of your soul, didn't this reality hit you like a two by four upside your head? This epiphany was practically like catching them doing it. Arghhh!

I sincerely believe this is when my lifelong battle with insomnia began.

# WHO-HE-HA

You would think that after working all day, Dad would come home and relax or collapse, especially at the prospect of dealing with five boys. Lord knows how many times Mom used that old expression, "Just wait until your father gets home!" in an always failed attempt to corral the posse of ingrates. Most fathers of the era came home to an easy chair, a cocktail waiting, and dinner in the oven. After a short homecoming greeting at the front door, children were shushed away so the man of the house could relax and unwind after a hard day at the office. But not our father, he was the original Energizer Bunny.

After a family meal, there would be chores to attend to. Well, we always had a list of chores he would leave for us, before going off to work every day. But there were some things he simply liked to do himself, and probably to blow off a little steam from work. Dad had a vision for our little place in the country, a plan on how to make it happen and the resources of five boys. Well, in fairness to the older three, us little guys only tagged along. We wanted to be a part of these grand projects…at least until our attention span ran out and we were back under the front porch playing with our Tonka toys.

One of Dad's favorite weapons of mass destruction was his coveted loppers—not a saw, chainsaw (too expensive for our blood), or an axe (too dangerous and inefficient). The loppers were the perfect tool for this man. With his incredible upper body strength and the cutting leverage of this tool, he could clear scrub brush and small poplar trees ('junk trees' according to Dad), from our ten-acre home site.

He had a vision of planting thousands of evergreen seedlings, mostly Blue Spruce and Norway pine trees, which would one day form a natural protective barrier around the house from the frigid winter winds. Arctic air blowing snow into huge drifts would literally cover over the front of our house. These were some of the coldest, harshest winters on earth, and no I'm not talking about Siberia, Alaska, or either of the Poles. No one and no place has any bragging rights over Duluth, Minnesota blizzards racing across Lake Superior.

Dad would grab the loppers and the boys would follow behind with rakes, wheelbarrow, and expressions of dread on their faces. He wouldn't stop moving from the time he lowered the working end of his loppers until he completed the planned clearing for the day, or the sun went down, whichever came first. He was like the Tasmanian devil from the Looney Tunes cartoons, cutting a swath of destruction through the scrub brush like a tornado.

Eventually, he would fall into a rhythmic pace, including his breathing. It was all through his mouth in what sounded like a three-step process of intake, hold and then exhale. And there was a very distinct sound he made in the process which in words appeared to be "who…he…ha…" While mostly it was the air rushing in and out of his lungs, there was a hint of verbal noise of some sort that blended into the mix. So now the Tasmanian devil is more akin to a steam engine getting underway and up to cruise speed.

"Who-he-ha…who-he-ha…who-he-ha…who-he-ha…" and on and on and on.

Like the little engine that could, the sound of lopping would start off slow and then pick up speed.

Well, you can imagine how the boys reacted to this development. Maybe it was the culmination of the really hard work, not knowing when or if Dad would ever stop and that horrid circumstance of trying not to laugh out loud.

"Who-he-ha…who-he-ha" …lope, lope…pick-up sticks…smirking eye contact between the boys… "Who-he-ha…who-he –ha" …lope, lope… smirk…giggle.

Repeat…giggle louder.

Repeat…giggle becomes laughter.

Repeat…uncontrolled mayhem, followed by Dad turning his head to give *the look* while not missing a loping beat…end humorous side trip, back to serious work.

This scene repeated itself many times throughout the years. Any project, large or small, that required sustained physical work produced Dad's song of "who-he-ha" followed by a chorus of laughter from the boys' choir.

To this day at family gatherings, we can't even say "who-he-ha" without breaking up.

The tree project continued for the entire first year of living in our new home on Swan Lake Road. Maybe longer, but not much, as Dad wanted to get the seedlings planted, and in Duluth one had a very short planting season before summer came to an end and the ground returned to a variant of permafrost. The short summers contributed to a glacial growth rate for trees in northern Minnesota. He knew we had to get them planted soon if he ever wanted to see them grow to maturity in his lifetime.

Many years later we all made it back up to Duluth for a family reunion. Of course, we drove by the old place on Swan Lake Road. The trees we planted were so tall and thick we could barely see the house through the gap of the long driveway. The entire home site was cradled by huge evergreens which, like Dad had envisioned, created a natural shield from the brutal winter storms. I'm certain that today a blizzard could be raging high above our little farm and yet you would think it was a tranquil winter day looking out the huge bay windows.

## SHOWER TIME

Our parents were Depression babies. Dad was born in 1928, Mom in 1930. They, like their entire generation, were greatly affected by the austerity and poverty of the time. As a result, nary a day went by when a parent, usually Dad, could be heard shouting, "Close the door, you weren't born in a barn," or "Turn off the lights, you're driving up the electric bill." They always seemed obsessed with saving every nickel, dime, and penny, especially when it came to the utilities. It was as if we were on the verge of going broke and losing the farm at any time…every day.

Water was no different, and when it came to bathing a bunch of dirty boys, we could run a few gallons through the meter. Thus, showers were the order of the day in our household. To make things worse, Dad had been in the Navy. Naval ships had to strictly control water consumption by the crew, as the supply was limited to the capacity of the onboard storage tanks. Thus, the term Ship Shower was born to describe the exact process and allotted time for sailors to shower while on board.

The process is simple. First, you get in the shower before turning on the water. No, you don't get to run the water until it warms up. Then turn on the water, get wet from head to toe, shut off the water, lather up, again from head to toe, turn the water back on, rinse off, shut off, and get out for the next person in line. Total time required not to exceed two to three minutes. Ship Showers were only for cleaning up, not relaxing after a hard day at work.

Care had to be taken not to open your eyes when your face was full of soap as you felt around for the knobs to turn the water back on. This may be okay when in a single stall, but not so good when in an open, locker room setup. Better be careful what 'knobs' you try to grab and turn with your eyes closed or you'll get punched in the face…or worse.

There were five boys (I think my older, teenaged brothers were spared as they already had this lesson) who after a day of chores and general farm mischief were dirty. "Filthy" was the term used most often by Mom as she directed us to disrobe down to our skivvies at the garage door before heading to the shower. Dad provided the instructions on how to properly take a shower. This was not a classroom lecture, rather a live demonstration. He lined us up in the bathroom, dropped trow, entered the shower and explained each step of a proper Ship Shower while actually taking one. Lesson completed, we each proceeded, one by one, into the 'classroom' to take a test shower and be graded by the instructor.

Now, there was no excuse for not knowing how to take a Ship Shower and the commensurate expectations for water consumption in the Gilbert house. As an aside, I'm pretty sure Mom was exempted from this rule for her sanity and Dad's wellbeing.

Naturally, if there was a way to improve something, Dad was the man to figure it out. The U.S. Navy couldn't possibly have found the best way to conserve water. He combined the effectiveness of the Ship Shower with the efficiency of Henry Ford's production line. When it was shower time, all able-bodied boys were ordered to the bathroom, where we disrobed and lined up. There we stood eyeballs to butt cheeks with Dad at the head of the line. The entire crew would follow him into the shower. Once the water was on, we would march forward, get wet, and circle to the back of the line. There we would lather up and then with eyes closed, mummy walk forward to rinse off. We exited at the front to avoid running into the next soapy dope in the line and have to rinse off again. Come to think of it, not only did the Old Man figure out how to wash five boys with even less water, but he also got to stand up front under the showerhead the entire time! Slick, eh?

## THE EVERYTHING CAN

*B*efore the advent of QVC-inspired products to organize and store everything in our lives, we had simple solutions using or reusing things right in front of our noses. One of these solutions could be found in literally every garage growing up. Dads around the country took empty food jars, cleaned them out, and used them for organizing and storing hardware like nuts and bolts, nails, screws, electrical bits and pieces. Most would simply set them on or under the ubiquitous workbench. Some would go one step further by mounting the metal lids to the underside of a wooden shelf above the workbench. Then with a twist, the jar hung at eye level. It was a simple, effective solution to organizing all the excess hardware normally kept for projects around the house, or in our case, the farm.

The clear glass jars provided an instant view of their contents with easy access. If Dad needed a screw, nut or bolt, all he had to do was eyeball the row of hanging jars, find what he needed, unscrew the jar, place it on the workbench, and get started on the project.

Naturally, there would always be various bits and pieces that didn't warrant their own jar. They were singles, unique, and oftentimes tossed in the garbage. But Dad didn't throw away anything. "You never know when you might need something like this," he would say. For all the little hardware misfits, there was the Everything Can. It was a one-gallon, restaurant size tin can. Cans that formerly held tomato sauce, canned fruits, and vegetables. With no top, it sat on the bottom shelf of his workbench. He would toss the extra odds and ends into the can without even looking. Eventually, the Everything Can was filled to the top.

To find something that wasn't in a hanging jar, you would always go to the Everything Can before heading off to the hardware store. The method was to first glance at the very top layer. If you were lucky, the right part for the job was laying right on top. If not, then with a brush of the hand, move the top layer around to stir up the hidden gem just beneath the surface. If that failed, you had to lift the now very heavy, densely filled can off the shelf and begin pouring out the contents a little at a time. The garage floor served nicely to move, sift, and search the odd mixture of stuff. It was like a hardware archaeological dig. We had fun competing to see who would be the first to find what Dad needed that day. Care had to be taken not to mix up the various piles so you wouldn't sift through the same stuff. Once the right piece for the job was found, we simply swept up the mess into a metal dustpan or small shovel and dumped it all back into the can.

One day, while Dad was at work, I had a bright idea. Dad had received a new, hand-cranked ice crusher for his birthday. This was the era of having "bumps" before dinner. JD was famous for his Manhattans. Manhattans require lots of crushed ice. I thought it would be nice to surprise Dad by mounting his brand-new ice crusher to the side of the kitchen counter where he always set up his bar. While it could be used atop the counter, that required a bit more force to hold it in place with one hand while turning the crank with the other. Mounting it would make the task much easier.

It came with a mounting bracket and wood screws. Seemed like a simple and straight forward project to me—pick the best location for the ice crusher, mark the spot for the bracket with a pencil, drill, screw, install. At the age of ten, I had already watched my father do so many projects using all his tools, and he was always teaching us kids along the way.

"Measure twice and cut once," he would instruct.

*He's going to be so happy with me.*

All went according to plan, until the final tightening of the screws. You see, watching our father do a project is not the same as doing one by yourself. The feel of the tools and the wisdom gained from experience and mistakes was why he could do anything with a few hand tools, some wood, and hardware…hardware from The Everything Can. Unfortunately, I still thought that if a little tightening was good, then more would be better. Big mistake!

Once the screws had pulled snug, I gave them a couple of extra turns just for good measure. Well, I went one turn too many and all three screws stripped right out of the soft cabinet wood. The entire bracket hung there, loose and wobbly.

"Crap," I said out loud.

*I'll just move the bracket over enough to drill new holes and cover up the mistake holes,*

I still had time before Dad got home from work. *Don't overtighten screws this time!* I scolded myself. Bracket successfully mounted the second time, I attached the crusher and stood back to admire my handiwork.

*Hmm, maybe I should give it a test run. Good idea, make sure it works properly.*

Dad always tested his work before he cleaned up and put away all the tools. So over to the freezer, grab an ice tray, remove a few cubes and drop them into the newly mounted crusher. Holding the lid firmly in place to prevent any ice from jumping out the top and hitting the kitchen floor, I began turning the crank. It was difficult; a lot of resistance, but it was working. "Yeah," I said under my breath. Smiling with pride, I continued to crank…one…two…three…wobble-zip-crash! The entire thing pulled right off the cabinet; hit the floor with a bang, and crushed ice flew everywhere.

*Oh God, oh God, what have I done?* screamed through my head. The horror and fear seared into my heart. Two sets of three holes glared at me from the cabinet. *Dad is going to kill me…worse; I'm going to get a spanking!* The fear and anxiety were debilitating.

Mom came running up the stairs from the laundry room. "What happened? Are you hurt?" she asked with urgency—typical of Mom. With a look of death upon my face, I explained everything to her. Unlike a couple of my siblings, I simply lacked the DNA to fib. She helped me clean up. We put the ice crusher back in its box except for the now bent and stripped screws. I tossed them into the Everything Can, and Mom smoothed over the six-pack of holes with her hand. Our plan…pretend as if nothing had happened.

Now, I literally had to wait until my father got home. What was to be a grand celebration had abruptly turned into a horror movie. I hid downstairs in the rec room. Mom went outside to hang laundry on the clothesline. It wasn't long before the station wagon turned off Swan Lake Road and headed up our long, gravel driveway. Dad was home.

I listened from below like a church mouse. I could hear the usual end of day back and forth between my parents. Then it hit… "What the hell happened here?" Dad asked with anger. "Well…" began a rather long and pleadingly empathetic explanation from my mother. Mom was always our lawyer. She was a self-appointed legal counsel for all cases of the State (our father) vs. her *always* innocent children. She was actually pretty good negotiating a plea deal with JD, especially on misdemeanor charges like messy rooms, chores not completed on time, etc. But felonies like destruction of State property were a different matter.

*STOMP, STOMP, STOMP*—I could hear and feel Dad's footsteps to the door atop the stairs. The door swung open with speed and purpose. "*JAY*, get up here right now!" he commanded. My legs were trembling so bad I could barely climb the stairs to the kitchen. "What, Dad?" I asked in my meekest, please have mercy, voice.

"What is this? What did you do?" he asked accusingly.

"I…I…I don't know," I responded in a miserable attempt to slither out of this mess. Mom had told him, but he wanted me to fess up-to tell the truth.

I didn't last long. I melted under the pressure like butter on a hot pancake. Oh, how I wanted a Dukie Cake at that moment. I'd rather be dead than face my father. Everything spewed forth, including why I did it. My intent dented his resolve for punishment a bit.

Still, a lesson had to be taught. "Look what he did, he's destroyed the cabinet," he said to Mom. "How did you let him do this?" he asked her. Oops—that was a mistake on Dad's part. It's one thing to accuse the perp, but to attack the defense attorney was over the line. Note to self, never rile up a Finlander's temper. The hard edges of Dad's anger were abruptly sanded down by Mom's…shall I say… passionate response. Perry Mason would have been proud.

Dad still pushed for a conviction but with a tad bit more compassion toward me. "Where are the wood screws?" he asked.

"They're in the Everything Can," I said. He told me to go get them. I knew if he saw them, all bent and threads stripped, the anger would return, and the scope of my failure would be fully exposed. I did find them, but I stalled.

"Did you find them yet?"

"No," I replied with anxiety. I kept shuffling metal

hardware around the basement floor as tears of shame ran down my face.

"Come on, Jay," he directed.

"But Dad, I can't find them," I responded, crying.

Now the tears were flowing like a river and dropping like a waterfall all over the soon to be rusty metal contents of the Everything Can. Dad kept insisting I find them. I kept shuffling nuts and bolts over the floor, and my crying elevated to full-on wailing. Finally, I could hear Counselor Mom say, "Stop, he's had enough now." Dad surrendered.

He came downstairs, assembled the proper tools and hardware, and proceeded to repair the damage, mount the ice crusher, and with me at his side, taught me how to do it right. The entire fix didn't take him more than fifteen minutes. Once done, he had me clean up the mess and put away his tools. Then, in his way to say, "case closed," he took some ice cubes from the freezer, put them in his new crusher and made a couple of his famous Manhattans for Mom and him. Raising his glass, he took a long pull of his drink, smiled at me, and with a wink, said out loud, "Smooth."

Dad's Everything Can was just a bucket of bolts to him. For me, it has become a symbol of the man, of a father. With his Everything Can, he taught us how to do everything. With his Everything Can, he showed me I could do anything. Dad's Everything Can was filled with honesty, integrity, and accountability. But most of all, his Everything Can was topped off with understanding, forgiveness, and love.

I can only hope I have given my sons their very own Everything Can.

# THE ELECTRIC FENCE DANCE

Pastures are open fields enclosed by fences. Fences for horses and cows are nothing more than heavy gauge wire—sometimes barbed—stretched and nailed to wooden posts. Our fences were about four feet high. They were high enough to hit a quarter horse in the chest and cows or ponies in the snout. There were two rows of wire to contain both tall and short livestock.

Both horses and cows would constantly test the fence for weaknesses in their never-ending quest to get to greener grass on the other side. On the farm, the grass really is greener on the other side. So how does one control a thousand pounds of hungry hooves pressing against a thin wire? Electricity, of course. The top strand was attached to glass insulators. These insulators were round and looked like long marshmallows with grooves around the outside and a hole in the center for a nail. They would be nailed to the fencepost and the wire was simply looped around the insulator and held in place by the groove.

Once the fence posts were in place—no small task, given the rock-laden Minnesota ground— the boys would pull the wire taut while Dad nailed insulators to posts. Starting at one side of the tack barn, running around the entire pasture, the circuit was completed by running the wire into the barn and connecting it to the electric fence box. This box converted 110-volt electricity into a safe level of pulsing electricity sent out along the entire fence line. It was strong enough to shock a fully-grown horse or cow off the fence they were attempting to breach.

You can imagine kids, especially boys, trying to get one or another to grab hold of a live fence. Yes, some brothers (older) would tell other brothers (younger) "Go ahead, touch it. It's not on." Have you ever experienced electric shock? Well, from firsthand, gullible experience, it hurts like hell! What's more, these things were designed to keep the fence clear by killing tall weeds that encountered the wire. In fact, the box we had was called the Weed Burner. The electric current was so strong that errant foliage would be dead within a couple of days after hitting the electrified fence. The box had two big lights, one green, and one red. The green light would go on and off in sync with the electrical pulse action. This indicated the fence was on and working. The red light meant something big, like a tree branch, or deer had hit and probably broken the fence or separated the wire from an insulator. In any case, that meant the fence was not electrified, and if not repaired, the animals would eventually figure it out and escape. Yes, they were dumb enough to keep trying even after being shocked.

One sunny, summer weekend day, Dad had the boys assembled next to the little barn preparing for some big project. There was always something to build, repair, or maintain on the farm. Horses and cows are hard on fences, barns, and gates. Whatever the project was that day, it required moving back and forth between the little barn and the fenced pasture. The big gate was…well…big. The wire fence was pliable enough to push down and hop over. It was common for Dad to simply cross between upper and lower strands of the unplugged fence. It was quicker than using the gate and eliminated the very real risk of hooved prisoners from escaping through a poorly latched gate.

What followed that day was an example of "if you want a job done right, do it yourself."

"Is the fence off?" Dad asked.

"Yes" someone replied.

"Are you sure?"

"Yup."

So, over the fence he went. Lifting one leg over, straddling the fence, it hit.

ZAP! ZOW! ZING!

"Y- E-O-W!" he screeched.

The fence shocked the Old Man right on his… um…manhood. To make matters worse, he always went commando on the farm, and he was wearing his favorite, well worn, pair of khaki work pants. So well worn, they had a hole right in the crotch. It couldn't have been his leg or thigh—no, it was dead center, hot wire to bare flesh.

Jumping straight up in the air and landing on the pasture side of the fence, he grabbed his crotch with both hands and started cursing at the top of his lungs. Every colorful metaphor in his vocabulary and even made up a few new ones we had never heard before rang out over the farm and beyond. Combinations of God, Jesus, and procreation spew forth in the form of verbs, nouns, and adjectives as he kicked up a cloud of dirt in a seizure-afflicted dance in between stunned horses and cows.

We all stared at the testicle spectacle for an excruciatingly long several seconds or so before the horror of the situation hit us. There was about to be some serious ass chewing and butt whooping.

"RUN!" someone yelled.

Fortunately, Dad was on the other side of the

electrified fence. We scattered everywhere and anywhere. Some of us ran back to the house and hid under beds. Others disappeared into the woods out back. It took him some time to calm down before coming after the culprit or culprits and dispensing the inescapable punishment. This was extremely good fortune for the guilty.

We never did find out who was responsible and if this was intentional or a simple mix-up of one kid thinking the other had unplugged the fence. But we would never forget the image of Dad getting zapped in the nuts and then putting on a set of moves that would make Michael Jackson look like an amateur.

That was the day The Electric Fence Dance was born.

# PLANTING DUCKS

Yes, you read that right. Planting ducks was an annual event born out of true conservation and a love of all thing's nature by our father. He never hunted or fished for anything he didn't plan to eat and taught us to never take more than we needed. Sure, there was the sport of hunting and fishing, but for him and what he instilled in us were the enjoyment, appreciation, and respect for nature, wildlife, of being outside instead of watching the 'boob tube.' In that spirit, every spring during mating season we would trek out to the marshlands, low areas of tall grass that bordered the lakes. As we got closer to the main body of water the marsh got wetter, with clumps of tall grass forming tiny little islands which eventually opened to small channels leading to open water. Since it was spring it was mostly brown, dead grass from the previous year with a smattering of green popping up here and there.

The first essential tool for part one of planting ducks was a long rope, usually made up of two horse lead ropes joined by the metal snaps. This was both effective and efficient as the metal snaps ended up in the center of the newly created rope, which helped hold it close to the ground. This was key to the process. The other thing required was a bucket or box lined with a soft bed of grass pulled from the location of the day.

We would set out to walk a field like a farmer harvesting wheat or corn, one large swath down; turn one hundred eighty degrees, return, and so on until we had covered the entire area. There would be one person at each end of the rope, holding it tight enough to drag over the top, if not somewhat through, the tall marsh grass. A couple more of us would form a line between the two ends and follow along. This operation would eventually flush a hen off her nest. We would collect her eggs, knowing that ducks will nest twice in the same season. It's nature's way of compensating for predators that would raid nests and eat the eggs. After a solid day of collecting duck eggs, we would bring them home and gently place them in an incubator—basically a box built of thick hardwood, with an insulated glass door, heater, and a light. The heater could be adjusted to mimic the body temperature of a nesting hen.

We watched it every day for signs of the ducklings hatching. Eventually, we would see the slightest little crack in an egg. Not a line, but rather more like a ragged hole which would grow larger with every peck of the duckling's beak. A beak which mother nature equipped with a hard tip, gave them the ability to crack the shell and create an opening large enough for them to eventually climb, fall, or stumble out of their shells. It would start with one, then another, and another. They seemed to all hatch on the same day within hours of each other.

Amazingly, they began peeping while hatching, as if looking for their siblings and cheering for one another to get out. There was a sense of urgency in their calling to each other during the hatch, as if they knew that they only had so much time to complete the task or they would die, and what had been their home, source of protection and food, could entomb them like a tiny round casket. Indeed, that's exactly what happened to a small percentage of every batch of eggs. "Nature's way of eliminating the weak," Dad would say. Now we would let them grow a bit. Let them get their legs under themselves, but not too long, as it was critical, we returned them to the marsh before they got too big.

You see, ducks will take in other ducklings along

with their own brood. But this needed to happen early on, say within a couple of weeks from hatching, as mother ducks will only adopt the orphans the same size and age as their own. They take them both literally and figuratively under their wings. For the rest of the summer, the ducklings would learn how to find food, avoid and hide from predators, and eventually, by example and a little prodding to stick with the flock, learn to fly. We would return to the very same place where we first collected their eggs with boxes of fluffy baby ducks. Rafts of ducks could be seen on the lake. The surrounding marshland was teaming full of hens with their hatchlings.

After placing the boxes on their sides in front of a small channel of water within the marsh, we would open the top and the entire brood would instinctively, if not awkwardly, waddle straight into the water. Peeping ecstatically, they began searching for their adoptive family. As suddenly as the first hen flushed off the very first nest we found earlier in the spring, the ducklings swam off, out of sight. They were gone.

Thus, at the end of the day, we had effectively doubled the number of ducks from every nest we raided and put back into the wild more than we ever took during hunting season. Other than taking in the scenery and appreciating the moment, it was a pretty matter of fact occasion. No sad goodbyes, they were ducks, and next season some of them might very well end up on our dinner table. This was simply good, sound conservation by replenishing the resources of nature.

# OH MY GOSH WINNIBIGOSH

The air was crisp and dried the inside of my nose. A few billowing clouds lumbered in the deep blue sky. Gold and crimson leaves littered the ground, a few still hanging on until a swift breeze breaks their final hold to a branch. Fall in northern Minnesota is beautiful, peaceful, yet ominous in its certainty to end with the first winter storm rolling off Lake Superior. Fall signaled the beginning of another religious event in northern Minnesota—duck hunting season. Migrating flocks were comprised of both mature birds and adolescents hatched just a few months earlier, young, strong, and eager to follow their elders south.

Duck hunting for us was not just about shooting or putting food on the table. We never took anything we didn't intend to eat. Rather, it was more about being outside, in nature with family. It was the challenge and skill of trying to hit a duck flying over a lake.

We arrived early at Lake Winnibigoshish (we called it Winnibigosh). Dad and one of my big brothers untied and lifted the Grumman duck boat off the top of the station wagon. It looked like a fat canoe with a square stern where we mounted the Johnson outboard motor. While that was going on, the rest of us unloaded all the hunting gear and staged it on the little wood dock.

Now, I've already described "necessary equipment" for the various Gilbert outings, but duck hunting has a few more items like big green canvas bags filled with decoys—decoys with lead weights for anchors—shotguns in cases, and a metal ammo can filled with shells. Oh, and don't forget the hundred pounds of Chesapeake retriever. Top it all off with life jackets, boots, gloves, camo hunting jackets over layers of clothes, and a cooler filled with sandwiches and pop and well, you can see the gross tonnage of the operation added up quickly.

This package of kids, guns, decoys, and dog worked fine for the early years when only the big three went hunting with Dad. But this trip included the whole family, which compounded the logistical challenge due to the Grumman's size and capacity. Our destination was Raven Lake. Raven was small, inconvenient, and off the beaten path. Most hunters were too lazy or impatient to make the trip, so we were likely to be the only hunters present. It can only be accessed by navigating across Winnibigoshish to a narrow, winding channel called Raven Creek.

Dad knew exactly where he wanted to set up on Raven Lake. With time on our side, he decided the safest way to get everyone from point A to point B was in two trips. Leaving one of the older guys with the little guys, he launched the now-loaded boat and set out for Raven with the other two brothers our Chesapeake Dukie, and all the gear. It was about a thirty-minute round trip, not including the time to unload and set up the decoys. Finally, we could see the little green Grumman speeding back across the big lake to pick us up. No sooner than he cut the engine and coasted up on the shore, we jumped on board and settled in for the second trip.

The run across the open waters of the Winnibigosh was laced with a small chop of waves that sprayed over the bow of the Grumman and hit my face with a cold sting. The fall air was crisp and fresh. Raven's Creek, on the other hand, was narrow and calm. Protected from the wind by tall marsh grass, its water was glasslike and reflected the fall colors like a huge mirror.

I must have been a dog in a previous life. I loved being outdoors, taking in all the sights, sounds, and smells. The most precious gift Dad gave to us all was an appreciation of nature…to look up, out, and around…to take it all in. To notice the hawk circling high above, the snowshoe rabbit hiding under a pine bough, a doe with her yearling trotting behind…to see what's right in front of your nose. This excited me more than the actual hunt. In fact, I would have preferred to go exploring.

The little boat settled down in the water as Dad slowed the Johnson. Calmly, we weaved through the winding channel; my eyes peered forward with anticipation for what might be right around the next bend. Then the water widened, and Raven appeared as if rising out of the marsh. Dad turned the handle on the Johnson, speeding us back up for a short jaunt to the spot he set up on the first trip.

Approaching the marsh, he slowed and then cut off the outboard. Coasting in, the boat pierced the tall grass surrounding the shoreline as we ran up on solid ground. Scurrying over the bow, we marched over to the area where the first group had set up for the hunt. It was a small, fat peninsula, which forced the migrating fowl to fly close to shore as they traversed the lake. The decoys had been set off from the point. They looked like a raft of ducks resting and feeding in the shallow water. Add to this Dad's skill with a duck call, and it was only a matter of minutes before an approaching flock was lured down to our spot. We sat still like kneeling statues. Camouflaged coats and pants hid our presence. When they were close enough, we would stand, pick a duck, and shoot. For the skilled and practiced, it was one smooth motion, usually followed by a big splash offshore as the bird hit the water. Duke would patiently wait for the command to retrieve them.

Dad was an excellent shot, bested by none of his peers, let alone his kids. Not that he wanted to beat us; in fact, he wanted us to be great shots like him. He always wanted us to shoot a duck, catch a fish, or bag a deer more for us than for himself. It was a rite of passage. A right I had yet to achieve, at least when it came to hitting a duck flying by at forty miles an hour. To add to the challenge, you had to identify what kind of duck was coming in before you pulled the trigger. Fish and Game would determine limits based on the estimated population of each type of duck. No, not all ducks quack or look alike. There were mallards, pintails, green wing teal, redheads, and canvasbacks, just to name a few. Dad could identify the exact breed by their wing beats and profile while they were flying. I only saw ducks.

After a few failed attempts, I was about to give up when a duck came swimming along right in front of my spot. Trying to remain calm, heart in my throat, I waited until it was well within range. Pulling my little 410-gauge shotgun—a small, lightweight gun for kids

—up to my ten-year-old shoulder, I took aim without even standing. Slowly squeezing the trigger, the round went off with a poof of smoke. It hit the bird, but not a clean shot. The little black duck rolled on its side, one foot flopping above the water. He just spun around in circles. Dad came running to see what happened, to see if I was hurt. He was genuinely concerned.

"Jay, are you okay? What happened?" he asked with urgency. "Did you drop your gun?"

He was alarmed by the shot, as there were no flying ducks at the time the little 410 went pop.

"I'm okay. Look, I shot my first duck!" I proudly announced. I was so excited. I wanted to please my father as this was important to him. Unlike my older brothers, I had yet to shoot my first duck.

Dad looked out over the open water. Upon seeing the wounded bird, I could hear him utter under his breath, "Oh shit." Then with a pained, yet forgiving look, he told me I had shot a Coot. Coots were illegal to shoot.

*Oh shoot, I shot a Coot!*

To make matters worse, I had shot him in the water. Another major booboo, as you're supposed to take them in flight, or "on the wing," as hunters say. I had committed two hunting no-no's all to join the time-honored club of bagging my first duck. Dad, in his merciful and conservationist way, raised his 12 gauge, took aim, and put the little duck out of his misery. To avoid any confrontation with Fish and Game, he left the Coot in the lake to float away. No retrieval for Duke this time.

My day of hunting had ended, not because Dad said I couldn't, but rather due to my embarrassment and self-inflicted shame. I sat quietly observing nature, as I did at home through the big bay windows.

As morning passed over lunch and into the afternoon, the sun began to lay low on the horizon. It was a beautiful fall day and a good hunt for the entire family—Duke included. But we pushed the time a bit too long. As we began to unload the shotguns and zip them safely in their cases, Dad realized we simply wouldn't have enough time for two trips back to the landing. In fact, a different look washed over his face…a look of concern. It was a look that caught our attention. He was doing the math in his head. We were in trouble.

Loading everyone and everything into the little green boat that a few hours before required two trips, would now push it deep down into the water. It would be impossible for the outboard motor to get it up to speed and on plane. Both of which would add stability and control, in addition to reducing the time to get back. The return trip would be painstakingly slow and dangerous. Dad assembled boys, the dog, and equipment like a puzzle…a puzzle where the weight of each piece mattered as much as fit. To further complicate matters, the Grumman had to be pushed out from the shore to allow it to float with enough draft with the extra load. We didn't need to get stuck in the mucky bottom. We had to board and load a floating, wobbly boat without the convenience of a dock. The last passenger carefully pushed off from the bow with a paddle and the Grumman slowly drifted backward into the calm, cold waters of Raven Lake. Dad smoothly pulled the Johnson to life and reversed us out to deeper water. An aura of quiet concern blanketed everyone. I tried to breathe quietly, as if that would help stabilize the boat.

His every move of the outboard was planned, purposeful, and made with extreme caution. No tight turns and little throttle more than idle. Any sudden turn, change of speed, or shifting of weight could push the low side beneath the surface, allowing the lake to pour in, swamping us in the cold, murky fall water. The water was so high on the gunnels it almost touched my overhanging nose.

Normally I loved watching the water pass by, captivated as the bow split it in two, curling lines creating a wake at the rear. But today it loomed large and ominous. Sitting on the bottom of the Grumman to help keep our center of gravity low, my nose inches away from the gunwale. Fixated on the twists and turns of Raven Creek as we navigated back to

Winnibigosh, there was no spying over the marsh for foxes, otters, or turtles sunning themselves on the shoreline.

Oh my gosh, it's Winnibigosh! Big, deep, and wide-open, it was angry with waves stirred up by the fall winds racing across from shore to shore. *How are we ever going to cross Winnibigosh? We're going to sink and drown to death.*

The little Grumman confidently made its way through Raven's Creek, pushed on by the Johnson to the big lake. As we made the final turn, the channel abruptly widened. Winnibigosh was dead ahead.

Entering the big lake, the wind hit us hard from the port side, momentarily pushing the Grumman over to starboard. Dad steadied us by turning into wind and waves. Freezing cold water sprayed across the bow and into our frightened faces. Coaxing the outboard a bit more gave us a hint of speed and stability, but making headway was still like living a slow-motion nautical nightmare. Wave by agonizing wave, each one seemingly intent on capsizing us, we pushed on.

The landing first appeared as a small spot off in the distance. It was discernible only because the manmade structure was a visual interruption in the otherwise wild and uninhabited shoreline. Nothing more than a gravel road running straight down to the lake, it had a concrete pad so boat trailers wouldn't get stuck, and there was a short, wooden dock on either side to tie up to while loading and unloading. Slowly, it grew into a recognizable place complete with boats, cars and, *yes…yes…there…I see them!* I screamed under my breath…people, real people on shore who could hear our cries for help and come out to save us if we sank.

They didn't notice at first, but then person by person, hunting group by hunting group, saw us approaching. Stares of amazement, concern, and a bit of "holy crap," met the dazed expressions on our faces. Sink we didn't, but the relief of knowing they were there was all I needed to feel okay. Dad pulled us into the protection of the landing. We were safe. *Would it be too much if I kissed the ground when I got out?* I wondered.

No time for celebrations. In his matter-of-fact way, Dad had us unloading the boat and hauling everything to the station wagon. With the Grumman secured upside down to the top and all the equipment loaded in the back, everyone jumped in their respective seats. "Smack, smack, smack" went the heavy steel doors of the Ford. He turned the ignition, put it in drive, and slowly pulled away on the gravel road. Winnibigosh disappeared out the tailgate window.

We all breathed a collective sigh of relief and sat quietly for a while as the car turned out onto the blacktop and headed for home. Then, like nothing special had happened at all, someone began recounting the day, pointing out excellent shots and brotherly kidding each other on the missed ones. There was no discussion of the boat ride, and no one mentioned the Coot. Smiles and laughter returned, but there was an air of thankfulness for our safe return home from Winnibigosh.

## DUKIE CAKES

By now, it shouldn't come as a surprise that we had dogs among our many pets. We had a Labrador and Chesapeake Bay retriever. In Minnesota, duck hunting was akin to religion. With ten thousand lakes and right in the middle of a major migratory pattern running from Canada down to the Mississippi to the Gulf States, we lived in duck hunters' heaven. In addition to all the required gear; shotguns, decoys, duck boat, camouflage clothes, and duck calls, you simply had to have a retriever.

Once the felled fowl hit the water, it was essential to retrieve them before they drifted away. Since flocks would come at a steady, if not unpredictable rate, it simply wasn't practical or efficient to have one of us get in the boat, paddle, or use the motor to run out to retrieve the bird. Further, the sight of a moving boat would scare the next flock away. Thus, it was essential to have a well-trained retriever. Large, strong water dogs such as Labradors and Chesapeake Bay Retrievers, better known as Chessies, were best suited for the cold water and waves whipped up by the stiff, fall winds. With their webbed paws, muscular builds, and naturally water repellant fur, they were known as big water dogs. They were loyal, kind, and extremely gentle, especially with children.

Our first retriever was a Chesapeake named Duke. Duke was a befitting name as he was large, muscular, well behaved, with a bit of a royal look atop his excellent posture. This was no couch potato of a dog. Chessies seemed to be serious and professional, whereas our Labs were happy-go-lucky goofballs. Yet, both dogs were all business when it came to duck hunting.

When the shotguns fired and the ducks splashed down, our retrievers would literally shake with excitement. But they wouldn't move a muscle until Dad knelt and held his hand straight alongside their head. Pointing in the direction of the downed duck, he would command "BACK" while flicking his hand. Instantly, the dog would burst into a full run and jump fifteen to twenty feet straight out into the frigid lake. Hitting the water with a huge splash, swimming with such strength and determination as to create a wake like a speeding boat, the retriever would bear down on the floating fowl like a laser-guided missile. Here's where the training and bloodlines really kicked in. Not only would he find and retrieve the bird, but he also did so with incredibly powerful jaws, filled with sharp canine teeth capable of ripping waterfowl apart in seconds, yet he never pierced the skin or pulled even one feather off the bird. Exiting the water straight back to Dad, he would sit, cradling the duck like a raw egg, and wait for the command "DROP," upon which he would let the dead duck gently roll out of his mouth into the hand of his master. If there were two or more ducks hit at the same time, the procedure was simply repeated until all birds were retrieved. With a well-deserved pat on the back accompanied by an affirming "good boy," Duke would shake off any remaining water, sit, and await the next flock.

We had a special bond with Dukie as both a respected hunting companion and beloved family pet. A strong, brave, dependable retriever he was a gentle giant with us kids, especially the babies. Putting up with us jumping on him, pulling his tail, and even lifting back his jowls to see his huge, sharp teeth, he'd lay there and take it without protest, as if it were his job. Dad would often lay us as babies between his huge legs, head upon his warm belly, paws gently wrapped around us in a protective swaddle. Like a warm, furry cradle, his chest would slowly rise and fall with each breath, rocking the infant to sleep. God help anyone who threatened to harm the baby! He was there for the birth of all five of us. We all were cradled and protected by him as infants. We had all bonded with him. We loved Duke.

One Sunday morning, late in Duke's life, we were enjoying our traditional Sunday pancake breakfast. Normally, Duke would sit next to the table as we gorged ourselves on the flapjacks smothered in warm maple syrup, hoping for something to *fall* off the table. On this morning he didn't get up. This was odd behavior, as he was still a dog and enjoyed treats from the table gods. Dad knew it was time. Earlier that week, Duke snarled and bared his teeth at one of us kids, likely from our usual goofing around with him. But this was simply unacceptable. Even in his old age, the dog could cause serious injury to a child.

Sensing the reality of Duke's condition, Dad looked his old friend in the eye with an assuring expression of love and respect. Duke looked straight back as if to say, "It's okay, my friend, I'm tired. It's time for me to go."

With that, Dad decided to make one last breakfast, fit for a king, for our family royalty…our Duke. He poured all the remaining dough onto the hot griddle. The huge pancake covered the entire surface. Paying special attention to cooking, taking care not to burn it, watching for the telltale bubbles indicating it was done and not raw inside, it rose thicker, higher, and bigger than any pancake we had ever seen before. Dad had to use two spatulas to flip it. We all watched in awe. All of us were excited and mesmerized. Dad was…well…different. Uncharacteristically quiet and a bit somber, he knew what had to be done, and it was dreadful.

Once the great pancake was done, he graciously, and respectfully, knelt and served his old pal the greatest breakfast a dog could ever dream of. Duke stiffly, yet energetically rose to his feet, eyes wide open, tail wagging, he tore into that pancake like a puppy. For those precious few minutes of his last meal, we had our old dog back. In that moment, he once again was full of life and joy.

Later that day, Dad loaded him into the back of the station wagon for his last trip to the vet. Gently laying Duke down on a warm, soft blanket, he shut the door and drove down our long, gravel driveway and out onto Swan Lake Road. Duke was gone. Tears flowed from my brothers and Mom.

When Dad returned from the vet he tried his best to explain to us little guys why Dukie wasn't coming home. We didn't understand. We were sad and upset.

Then from the mouths of babes rang, "You killed him! You fed Dukie that huge pancake and he died!"

"No, son, the pancake didn't kill Duke," Dad said with empathy. The look on his face was one of surprise with a little pain in his furrowed brow.

"No…YOU killed Dukie. If he didn't eat that pancake, he'd still be alive," we protested. Dad seemed perplexed if not a little hurt, but his reaction was calm and understanding. He knew this too would pass with time. Some things you can't explain to a child. This is how kids dealt with the incomprehensible. They had to have an answer to "why?" One they could understand.

From that day on, we blamed that damn pancake for killing Duke. Thus, was born the term "Dukie Cakes." Years later, when we could all laugh about it, we would jokingly threaten to make some Dukie Cakes for anyone who misbehaved. Today, they are an honor to make and receive…unless you're old, in which case you might want to pour yourself a bowl of cereal instead.

## DEADHEADS

One thing all Minnesotans have in common is fishing. Hey, with 10,000 lakes staring you in the face every day, what else do you think people up in "God's Country" do to pass the time?

In any event, Dad loved the outdoors. The only thing better was being outdoors with his boys. I also believe he knew Mom needed a break from the *animals,* and I don't mean the ones out in the pastures and pens! After a full day's work, he would haul ass home, load the station wagon with rods, reels, tackle box, fishing net, life jackets, and the Johnson outboard motor. Jesus, that thing was heavy!

Mom would have us ready to go when he got home so we would have as much time as possible to fish before sundown. Of course, Duluth, being so far north, was almost like Alaska—land of the midnight sun. With everyone and everything piled into the car, we headed down the driveway, right onto Swan Lake Road, cut over to Krueger Road, and then left onto Rice Lake Road. It was a short fifteen-minute drive to Rice Lake. Our fishing trips would begin at Martels Bait and Tackle, where Dad would buy minnows for bobber fishing, Nut Goodies (our favorite candy bar), and rent one of those old wooden fishing boats that had been painted dark green so many times, I didn't know if we were floating on wood or paint. Transfer everything from the car to the boat, prime, choke, and pull the old Johnson to life, and run the whole operation across the lake to the "deadheads"—the perfect spot to catch Walleye.

Running at full throttle, the heavy wooden boat, loaded with kids and gear, barely made it up on plane. In fact, it was more like a fast-moving tugboat. Nevertheless, with the crisp wind in our faces and the anticipation of catching the big one, we looked like a bunch of dogs sticking our heads out the car window, noses high and tails a-wagging. This was pure joy and happiness…until we sighted the deadheads.

Deadheads are simply trees that had died due to the raising of the water level from the lake's dam. Stripped bare of all life, no bark, leaves, or even small branches, some remained standing like the water's scarecrow. Some were leaning almost parallel to the water, creating a perch for ducks, birds, and turtles.

But most lay just beneath the surface, waterlogged, yet still buoyant enough that the wake of a passing boat would joust them alive from their watery grave, moving up and down as if to warn boats not to come closer or you will be sunk. The mere term deadhead and the close-up experience of rowing through them makes me shudder to this day, let alone when I was a kid.

Slowing to an idle, we entered the deadheads with caution. Dad would cut off the motor, letting the boat glide silently into the minefield of dead trees. The only sound was the water lapping on the sides of the ol' wooden boat. He had the poles readied for casting with Bassarenos—a fishing lure about two inches long, painted white with a red face and two, three-pronged hooks, front and back. They attracted walleyes like sharks to blood in the water. All he wanted was for his boys to catch fish, but my brothers were screwing up everything, backlashes, tangling each other's lines, and hooking everything but fish. Dad said "Give me a damn rod! I'll show you how it's done."

He put me in charge of rowing. He told me "pick a path between the deadheads and slowly, quietly, row in a straight line." He knew I could do it. He trusted me to get the job done. He probably knew I was afraid of the deadheads and rowing with a duty would be a distraction. It was.

Everyone but Dad was sitting. My brothers, in the front, were looking back over me, watching him. I was in the center of the boat, facing aft, but my eyes were focused on the lane of water behind us. Having picked an open path ahead, rowing in a straight line was a simple matter of watching the water move along the side and away from the boat. It flattened the ripples into a shiny ribbon. If the ribbon was straight, then I was rowing straight ahead. If it started to bend left or right, then we were turning. Gently, I pulled on the oars. Applying equal strength and cadence kept us on course and slowly, quietly moving through the deadheads. Special attention had to be paid not to hit any of the passing deadheads with an oar. The impact would cause both a missed stroke on that side of the boat and a sudden turn in the direction of the paddle run afoul. Worse, the clunking noise would scare the fish away. If I noticed even the smallest veering to the left or right, I would get us back on course with a little more pull on the opposite paddle. About every third or fourth stroke, I would turn my head enough to look forward and plan for any course correction.

Standing in the back of the boat, Dad picked a spot next to a submerged deadhead and cast the Bassereno with purpose and perfection. It landed with a splash like a frog jumping into the water right next to the deadhead. Not on it, in it, or over it, but right in the perfect spot where he knew a big ol' lunker would be waiting in the dark shadow of the dead tree. We all held our collective breath as he let the lure float, motionless for a few seconds before he started reeling it back in. Then, as he began to reel—*WHAM*— a walleye hit the bait so hard, both bait and fish erupted straight up and out of the water and then back down with a giant splash. The fight was on.

The pole bent like an upside-down U, the line fed out with resistance from drag set to tire the fish, but not let the line break under the pressure. Dad fought him in next to the boat, where he instructed one of my brothers to lower the big, round fishnet on a pole under the exhausted fish and lift it into the boat. Quickly and efficiently, Dad removed the lure, secured the fish to the stringer and dropped it over the side to keep them alive until we headed back to Martels.

Well, if one lesson is good, surely two would be better. The quickness of the first didn't really allow for good instruction on proper casting techniques. Once again, Dad surveyed the deadheads as I continued to calmly and quietly row down the chosen path. He stood, picked his spot, and cast to a new, unique place in the minefield at a completely different angle, yet with the repetitive precision of a well-oiled machine that had done this a thousand times before. Once again—*WHAM*—another hit, another fight, another walleye in the boat.

Smirking a bit, I could see he was having fun and really enjoying the moment. I don't know if he wanted to continue teaching or to keep fishing himself as he was on a roll, but *what the heck*, could be seen in his eyes as he made one last cast while fishing school was still in session. Yup, you guessed it. Three consecutive casts, three perfect placements in the deadheads, three huge walleyes caught. We all went crazy! My brothers were stupefied. Even Dad was surprised. Everyone was laughing, yelling, and demanding a pole.

Dad looked straight at me, smiled and in front of my brothers, complimented me on rowing a "perfect" path.

My heart filled with pride.

# ICE FISHING

Many years after leaving Minnesota, and well into my career, I had to make a business trip to Minneapolis in the dead of winter. Upon landing at the airport, the pilot jokingly announced "Welcome to Ice Station Zebra. The local temperature is twenty below zero." And that was without the wind chill factor! Further, Minneapolis was considered 'warm' by Duluthian standards.

My mind tried to recall what twenty below felt like as I made my way through the terminal to ground transportation.

As I exited the automatic doors to catch a cab, I inhaled the frozen night air for the first time since childhood. I was literally stunned to a halt by the instant burning sensation in my lungs. Then my face reacted. It was like walking straight into a brick wall.

Memory recall was complete, and the first thought that ran through my head was *how the hell do people live here?* completely forgetting the fact that we once lived here.

Unlike many parts of the country where winter is relatively short and people put up with it until springtime, in Minnesota it's so long and so cold the natives must adapt or go stark raving mad from cabin fever. The local joke was summer came on July 1st and ended July 2nd. Don't blink or you'll miss it. In fact, we could walk a few hundred feet into the woods and find hard frozen snow still lying under the dense canopy of the pine trees—in June! Thus, outdoor activities didn't stop with the arrival of winter in Duluth. Only the toys, gear, and clothing changed.

Ice fishing was the main source of frozen fun. In fact, it's more akin to a form of religion in these parts. At some point, after the mercury slid below freezing and stayed there for the next four to five months, some government officials would test and declare the ice safe to drive on. Yes, you heard that right, DRIVE ON! I guess if it was safe enough to drive a car over, it was safe for people to walk, skate, sled, and ride snowmobiles.

This much-anticipated event was greeted with great fanfare and excitement. It was broadcast on the radio, the local nightly TV news and made the Sunday paper headlines. The race was on for those with ice houses to pull them out over the lake to their secret fishing hole before anyone else staked a claim. Funny how the middle of almost all the "10,000 Lakes" had secret honey holes in the same place, resulting in mini Gold Rush towns of ice houses. Some of these shacks were more like cabins, complete with heaters, chairs, and cabinets stocked with food and drinks. They provided all the creature comforts of home and protection from the brutal cold and wind. But ice houses were for the well to do.

The Gilbert icehouse came in the form of our 1960 Ford station wagon, the original SUV. Like any other fishing trip, we would load the car with all the necessary gear, sans the Johnson outboard—no boats for ice fishing. One critical piece of equipment was the ice auger. Like an oversized, old fashioned hand drill, the auger was used to drill a hole in the ice about a foot in diameter. It was through these holes we would drop our baited hooks with a bobber floating in the constantly refreezing opening. It was so cold the holes froze over right before your eyes. This required the second most important tool, which essentially was an oversized ladle with holes that would be used to skim off the newly formed ice, allowing bobbers to float freely and announce the nibbles of fish below. The actual fishing was simple as they were very slow and lethargic due to the ice-cold water.

I'll never forget sitting in the *way back* of the

station wagon, behind the backseat, looking over the seats and out the windshield as Dad drove down the snow-covered road to Rice Lake. It was a wide-open expanse of blinding white, with little dots scattered about and a bunch clustered in the middle. The dots were ice houses. No stopping at Martel's Bait Shop to rent a boat. The car kept moving straight down to and out on the lake. Only a month ago we were speeding across this very same place in a boat heading for the deadheads. Now we were in two tons of Detroit steel, driving on an already plowed and worn ice road over the lake. Strong as steel, the ice nevertheless would groan and make cracking sounds as the car passed over it.

I always worried we would break through the ice and go straight to the bottom. It didn't help that every year some idiot would push the limits and go out one more time before the ice melted. They would crash through, their car or snowmobile too heavy for the weakening ice. Sometimes an entire family would be lost. The news would send shockwaves through the community. There was sorrow and sadness for the children, disdain, and ridicule for the parents—especially the dad. It's one thing for a drunken idiot on a snow machine to go through, but an entire family really hit home. This reality was on my mind every time we rolled out onto the ice.

Did you know that if you fall through the ice, look

for the dark spot? That is where the hole is, probably the one you fell through. Ice reflects light, especially sunlight, like a mirror. Assuming you have the presence of mind to do so while you're drowning to death, all you'll see is white, except for the hole. No light means no ice, so swim for that spot to save yourself. This little factoid was actually taught in the Duluth school system—a fact that only heightened my fear of driving on the ice. I can't say I shared my father's enthusiasm for ice fishing.

But once we were all set up, the actual catching of fish was fun and we would fill the time between plunging bobbers with ice skating, snowball fights and making snow angels. If we were lucky, Dad would start the car and turn on the heater to let us warm up a bit. Not too long though, as he knew it's hard to constantly go from cold to hot and back again. We had on so many layers of clothing that sweating was a real concern. Sweat is just water, and it would instantly freeze when we got back out of the car. This would only make it worse and could be dangerous, as frostbite was always a very real risk in subzero weather.

Layers upon layers of clothing were painstakingly put on to protect us. It was bad enough to be outside the house next to our wall of pine trees, which provided shelter from the wind, but exposed in the middle of a frozen lake was nuts. The wind, which could drive the temps to forty or fifty below, would race unabated across the flat, frozen lake. Exposed skin can incur frostbite in a matter of minutes. Our feet were covered with two pairs of socks; one made of cotton, the other heavy wool, all shoved into special, thermal lined boots. The rest of the body was equally wrapped up with long underwear, sweaters, pullover hoodies, and long, thick parkas. Hats, gloves, mittens, and scarves completed the project. We were walking mummies. I don't know how we ever managed to hold a fishing pole.

It was hard enough to get bundled up in the comfort of the house before going out to play. Ice fishing meant we had to keep the final layer, plus hats, mittens, and scarves off during the ride up to the lake. When Dad stopped the car, we had mere seconds before he opened the liftgate to begin unloading the gear. With the gate wide open, the polar air exploded into the car, evaporating any remnants of heat. We were squirming like a pile of worms, grasping for snow pants, parkas, wool hats, and anything else that might provide some protection from the elements.

Once fully dressed, we rolled out of the station wagon like a horde of Stay Puft Marshmallow men. No sooner had we hit the ice, than Dad was barking orders to get everything organized as he began drilling the holes. The blade end of the auger looked like one of those WWII folding army shovels, but a bit wider and more rounded. It was designed to move the ice shavings up and out, but as the hole got deeper, you would have to lift it out, clear the hole by hand, and then resume drilling. Once it began to pierce the bottom, lake water would fill the hole and combine with the shavings to make a huge slushy. Care had to be taken at this point. The final breakthrough happens fast, and if you don't hold on, the auger will drop right through the hole to the bottom of the lake. More than tackle boxes, fishing lures, and boat anchors combined, there must be thousands of these things scattered about the bottoms of Minnesota's lakes.

We would fish until we had our limit or lost feeling in our hands and feet, whichever came first. Even Dad wasn't immune to the extreme cold. Unless it was a sunny day with little or no wind, which with all the layers of clothing made it feel warm, ice fishing trips were short compared to summer days in a boat.

Still, it got us out of the house, away from the TV, and burnt up our pent-up energy. But most of all, we spent time together as a family.

## AND OTHER FROZEN FUN

*L*earning how to ice skate was like learning to walk in Duluth. In fact, most of us were put in skates as we were learning to stand. Learning how to play hockey was yet another a rite of passage in Minnesota and playing Pee Wee hockey was an integral part of the local culture.

While the sport is relatively expensive to play in most parts of the country due to the cost of building enclosed ice rinks, it was relatively cheap in Duluth. All you needed was a clear, flat space the size of a regulation hockey rink, the 'boards,' which are assembled like a solid rectangular fence with rounded corners, and water. Start watering with a fire hose and Mother Nature takes care of the rest. Flood, freeze and repeat until you have a nice, thick piece of ice covering the ground inside the boards. It was so cold that steam could be seen rising from the liquid water as it met the subzero air. The dads/coaches would complete the job by making the red and blue lines of a hockey rink using a chalklike powder and then seal it in with one final coat of water. *Voila*, you have a hockey rink. There was no need for a Zamboni machine to resurface the chewed-up ice between games. The coaches pulled out an old fire hose and flooded the rink. The water literally froze over in minutes. Next to the rink was a heated clubhouse which essentially served as a locker room for the teams. It had a concession stand. Hot cocoa was the best seller. We played for the Duluth Heights Hockey Club.

Hockey, like ice fishing, was played no matter how cold it got. Only a blizzard could stop play and force everyone inside. There are three periods in each game. The Pee Wee periods were shorter than the official length the teenagers played. Hockey skates are very stiff, with little insulating properties. Even with a couple pairs of socks, the cold penetrated right through and deep into your feet. A typical game went something like this; arrive at the clubhouse all suited up in uniforms, helmets, unbuckled, atop heads, and your skates skewered through the space between the blades and carried over your shoulder like a hobo's belongings. Sit down on a wooden bench, toss off your boots, and slide your feet into the skates. Now, this was a two-person job for us little guys. We were so bundled up and the uniforms had protective pads everywhere, including shoulder pads just like the ones worn in football, we could barely bend over. Tightening and tying the laces required parental help. Oh, another little tidbit that didn't help with the freezing cold was the fact that hockey skates must be laced so tight that they could, and often did, cut off circulation to your feet. This is what made the skate a sturdy extension of the legs. Straight ankles meant all the power went to the blades and provided force directly to the ice, which resulted in motion. Once ready, don your Hulk-like hockey gloves, grab your stick, and head out the locker room door to the rink. When the ref blew the whistle to end the first period, both teams made a mad dash for the warmth of the clubhouse. Stumble over the concrete floor covered with thick rubber mats to protect the sharp edges of our blades and collapse back down on the bench. Moms and dads would immediately remove our skates and instinctively begin rubbing our feet, which had become numb from the cold and lack of circulation. As the blood began to flow and the heat of the locker room started to warm the skin, you would feel a tingle. The tingle would quickly proceed to pain, followed by extreme burning. The entire Pee Wee team would be in tears, but this had to be done or we could get frostbitten feet and toes. Once the pain had subsided and the tears wiped away, it was time to lace up again and go back out for the next period. The cycle of play, freeze, thaw, cry, and play again had to be endured three times every game for the entire season!

But hey, this was "FUN!"

## PUSSYFOOTING

Living in the country surrounded by wilderness and having a father who loved to hunt, and fish meant we were outdoors, and often in the woods. Dad had the instincts of an Indian. He knew how to hunt, trap, and walk through the woods, and he was always teaching us kids. Whether hunting for Ruffed Grouse or sneaking up on deer, we had to pussyfoot. Unlike the dictionary definition *of avoiding a conversation, topic, or issue*, this pussyfooting was a specific way to walk through the woods without making noise.

To do this, you have to first watch where you are walking to not step on a stick that would crack and scare the animals away. Then pick a clear path through the woods to avoid scraping up against bushes, branches, or tall weeds to avoid making noise. Pussyfooting entails rolling your feet from the outside in, front to back with legs flexed or bent a bit in a way that prevents a straight down stomping action. Feeling for anything that might break underfoot, you can literally walk through the woods while barely making any noise. It's like tiptoeing with your whole foot.

Dad would always lead the way, with us kids following in line right behind. When he spotted something, he would stop, crouch, and hold out a hand, pointing down, palm open silently, indicating for us stop in our tracks. Then he would flick that same hand with a forward motion. We would move up right behind him to see what he spotted. If we were hunting that day, one of us got to move up to his side and under his guidance, take aim and shoot.

Silently pussyfooting through the woods was more exciting than a wild noisy snowball fight. You never knew what you would run into right around the bend or over a small hillcrest. The challenge was to see them before they saw or heard you. Sometimes, Dad would place us along an old tote road and then circle around to move game toward us. Always aware of our location when hunting, he would seemingly appear out of nowhere, but in a way that let us know he was there without alarming us. Usually, an intentional crunching of a stick underfoot or clearing of his throat would announce his presence. Then you realized he had been there for some time, and you didn't know it.

One summer afternoon, we were across the road in a clearing we used for our annual bonfire from hell. Just beyond was a thick underbrush penetrated by bear paths. They looked like big round tunnels winding through the woods, dark and damp. Dad decided to do a little pussyfooting down one of the paths with us in close formation on his heels. We hadn't gone more than fifty yards into the thicket when we discovered and practically stepped in a fresh pile of bear crap. So fresh it was still steaming and stunk to high heaven.

I can count on less than one hand the number of times I've seen our father scared. This was one of those times. We could hear it in his voice and see it on his face! Now when your dad, your bigger than life protector from all things bad in the world, says in a hushed, yet urgent way, "We need to get out of here right now!" you almost crap your own pants.

The bear was way too close for comfort and Dad was very concerned we would get between a mother and her cubs. This was a dangerous situation. We hightailed it back down the path, pussyfooting be damned. My heart was in my throat. The fear was almost debilitating. I thought for sure the bear was about to jump out of the underbrush at any second.

Dad brought up the back of the line to protect his boys.

Those were the longest fifty yards of my life. Once we hit the clearing, we kept moving, past the huge pile of drying brush, across the road, and literally ran up the driveway to the house. I didn't feel safe until the door slammed shut behind us. We didn't see any bears, but we stayed on our side of the road for a couple of weeks.

We did, however, answer that age-old question that summer's eve.

"Does a bear shit in the woods?" You're damn right it does!

## **NEVER NAME YOUR FOOD**

*V*irtually all the animals we raised for food were nameless, impersonal creatures. The chickens were especially easy to see as nothing more than walking, clucking, feathered food. Except for Ted, they *were* dumber than a box of rocks. When it was time for plucking and plating, it was easy peasy—at least for us humans. In addition to all the feathered foul, we had several cows. We named a couple of them Snowflake and Molly Brown. Snowflake looked like a patchwork quilt of white and black. Her white patches looked like snowflakes. In Duluth, everything seems to look like snow in one form or another. She was a Holstein hybrid. Holsteins are dairy cows, but Snowflake was also bred for meat.

Molly Brown on the other hand, was a Hereford which are bred for meat. They have no other purpose. Unless, of course, you give them names, raise them from calves, chase them around the pasture, and occasionally jump on their backs for a wild, bucking ride. They were about the same size as the Welsh ponies, but disproportionally fat and round.

We connected with Snowflake and Molly Brown like we did with the horses and ponies. In fact, they were more docile and laid-back creatures. They loved to be scratched behind the ears and right under their necks. When you hit the right spot, they would extend their heads outward and stretch their necks. It was like they were saying "Oh yeah, right there, a little to the left…ahh, that feels so good." Naturally, with all our loving care, alfalfa hay, and molasses covered oats, they grew fast.

Dad was no different in his affection for these cute bovines. I think he loved them as much as us kids, but he had to feed five boys. Sure, we bought most of our food from the grocery store. But it wasn't uncommon for county folk to offset the food bill by growing vegetables in a big garden, chopping heads off chickens and butchering a cow each year. If you had the land, you raised some cattle for meat.

When Snowflake was fully grown, it was time. She was put in a trailer and hauled off to the butcher. She returned to us in many packages wrapped with white butcher paper and labeled 'T-bones, porterhouses, ribeyes, filets, and hamburger.' Everything went into a huge freezer in the basement.

When it came time for our first Snowflake meal, all of us kids sat in silence looking at the sizzling steaks on our plates. "I'm not eating," one of us protested.

"Neither are we," the rest of us chimed in. "We loved Snowflake. Why did you have to kill her?"

Dad told us he gave Snowflake to a family as a pet. We didn't buy it. Then he said in a matter-of-fact tone, "You can eat this steak or go to bed hungry. I don't care." Then, he dug right in. Being so physically active outdoors, he was a voracious eater. We continued our vigil with stomachs growling and listening to Dad chewing and swallowing the juicy, delicious steak. To those sitting next to him, he would say "Are you going to eat that?" and before the upstart had a chance to answer, he would stab the steak with his fork and put it on his plate. At this sight, the rest of us protestors immediately broke ranks, picked up our forks and knives, and started eating. We didn't know how many steaks Dad could consume at one time, but we weren't about to find out, lest we lost our dinners as well.

It didn't take but a couple of meals to stop seeing Snowflake at the dinner table and start seeing T-bones and ribeyes.

Moral of the story: NEVER name your food!

## HATCHET JOB

My brother Jeff, third from the top, loved to antagonize and was always finding ways to get out of his chores. He loved to torment me. Being the quiet, timid one, made me easy prey. My brother took great joy in getting under my skin and sending me into fits of hysteria.

One of his favorite tactics to drive me bonkers was making dinner. Mom got a job selling clothing at a friend's high-end shop in downtown Duluth and needed some help around the house. Jeff always wanted to try something new and different. *The Galloping Gourmet* was on TV back then, and I think this was his inspiration. He would proceed using every pot, bowl, and utensil in the process. Further, he would intentionally make a huge mess. Eggshells, flour, salt, and pepper were tossed about the kitchen, including the floor. He knew I was a neat freak and used it to provoke me. From making my bed like I was in the military, to cleaning the toothpaste tube and properly squeezing it from the bottom, I wanted everything in its place, clean and tidy. Okay, so maybe I was a little obsessive-compulsive as a child. Jeff knew this was an easy button to push.

Once done with preparing dinner, he would command me to clean up the kitchen before Mom got home. I dutifully complied, given my aforementioned idiosyncrasies and wanting to make Mom happy. She didn't need to come home to a mess after working all day. To help, I would wade into the culinary catastrophe and proceed to wash, wipe, and mop. With everything cleaned up and all the pots, pans, and utensils back in their proper places, I would peer over the kitchen, taking stock with pride in my work. Then I would retreat to my big blue pillow in the living room for some well-deserved R & R.

That's when right on cue, Jeff would re-enter the kitchen to make dessert. Immediately and quite intentionally, he would open every cabinet door, remove every pot and pan regardless of need, and set about destroying the kitchen, and all my hard work, within minutes. He knew the reaction it would evoke from me, and I always delivered Oscar-winning performances straight out of a blood-curdling horror movie. I would scream so hard my voice would go hoarse. While tears flowed down my face, he stood there and ate it up with the grin of a Cheshire cat. Jeff's crime didn't warrant my overreaction. It was just a big brother antagonizing his little brother as they always have throughout time. But his behavior would ultimately come home to roost.

One sunny summer day, Dad had left his daily list of chores. Jeff's big job for the day was to cut the branches of a pile of small pines we had cut down over the weekend. Everything that met its fate at the working end of the loppers and handsaws ended up stacked into a huge pile that would eventually become our annual bonfire from hell. Farm refuse and burnable junk included things like old chicken coups, rotten fence posts and broken shovels or pitchforks. In order to pile an otherwise short, round evergreen, the branches had to be cut from the trunk, or they would simply roll off the pile.

Naturally, as soon as Dad drove down the driveway and out onto Swan Lake Road, Jeffery immediately switched from obedient son to master overlord. He turned and gave me the extremely sharp hatchet (think small axe with a short handle) and instructed me to start cutting off the branches. I was way too young and small to safely do this job, but as usual, I complied, as I didn't want Dad to be mad when he got home after work. I hated conflict with a passion—still do.

I began the task with Jeff sitting on his lazy behind and keeping an eye on me to ensure I kept working. Holding the small tree upright with my right hand and hatchet in my left, I would cut off the branches working from top to the bottom. Hatchets, like axes, work best with a full swing right to and through the branch. You don't try to stop it once the cut is made, as that would take momentum away. This resulted in one clean cut for the smaller branches up top and only a couple of strikes to remove the larger ones at the bottom.

Of course, I was barefoot to boot. We never wore shoes in the summer, except for church, riding horses, or shoveling poop out of the barn. After the first two or three saplings, my left hand, the one wielding the hatchet, started to get tired. My grip was getting loose, and the swings became erratic and uncontrolled. I was starting to flail at the next tree. Near the bottom, feet squarely beneath the last branch, I swung, missed it, and drove the sharp hatchet straight down into my left big toe. The pain was excruciating. The sight of the blade penetrating deeply into my toe was horrific. Blood gushed everywhere. My screams of pain and anguish echoed throughout the otherwise tranquil countryside. Birds flew from trees, the horses and cows perked their ears straight up and turned their heads toward the wails, chickens ran to the protection of their coop.

My howling rang through the house and brought my oldest brother, John, and his friend running out to my aid. Jeff had a look of "oh shit…I'm in deep trouble" plastered on his otherwise smug little face. John took control of the situation. "Get some clean rags" he commanded Jeff, who for once did exactly as he was told.

While I lay on my back in the pile of pine boughs, wincing back and forth in a sticky mixture of sap and blood, Johnny pulled the hatchet from my foot, wrapped the gaping wound with a rag, and applied pressure. Lifting me up with care, he carried me to his buddy's souped-up '57 Chevy. Laying me down in the backseat, he sat with my foot in his lap and told him to get us to the emergency room— *fast*!

"GO MAN GO…DRIVE!" he shouted.

Well, that's music to a teenager's ears. On a mission to save my life…err…big toe, His buddy *had* to drive fast. It was his duty to God and country to haul ass down Swan Lake Road to the hospital. The '57 roared to life. Holley four-barrel carb pumping loads of high-octane gas into the 283 small-block. With headers and glasspacks, that thing was loud. He shifted into first gear, revved the engine, and dropped the clutch. The rear wheels spun, leaving two carved gullies in the gravel driveway followed by a billowing cloud of dust. Swinging out on Arrowhead, a long, straight ribbon of asphalt, he laid rubber, creating another cloud, this time of white smoke with two black stripes tattooing the road until the tires finally gripped the surface and the car rocketed forward. The smell of burnt rubber filled the car.

The speedometer hit a hundred and kept rising. We were going so fast that John, a hellion himself behind the wheel, barked once again to his friend, "Take it easy, man, he's not dying."

Wow, even my big brother was scared! I thought it was fun, and as a side benefit, it distracted me from my toe.

The ER was not a common place for us, as improbable as that may seem for five boys on a farm with pitchforks, shovels, saws, and hammers. It took a serious injury to justify the expense. Mom would usually make sure there were no protruding bones or gushing arteries, patch us up, and send us back outside to play or complete our chores. Upon our arrival, the doctors and nurses went about their procedures, numbing, cleaning, and stitching my toe back in place. John got ahold of Mom at work, filled her in on the incident. When we arrived back home, she was comforting and understanding to me, but she only had one thing to say to Jeff. "Wait 'til your father gets home!"

# AUTHOR'S NOTE

On Saturday, September 24, 2016, two days after drafting this story, my brother Jeff, was found dead in a public park by the Metro D.C. police. He was homeless.

I struggled over whether I should include this story in an otherwise upbeat and fun book. But this memory is as fresh in my mind as the day it happened. It's a part of who I am.

I still bear the scar on my toe. Before, it was a reminder of something painful both physically and emotionally. With his passing, it is now a reminder of a brother I lost years ago…many years before his death…a bittersweet reminder that I had a brother named Jeff.

He was family, and now he's gone.

Rest in peace, dear brother.

Run free and happy again, back home on Swan Lake.
Jeffery Paul Gilbert

October 22, 1954 – September 24, 2016

# SALTIES

Duluth is a beautiful city built on the side of a steep hill that drops down to the head of Lake Superior. In its heyday, the city was a bustling international seaport and home of the great ore docks where the lake freighters (ore boats) were loaded with iron ore. The port was so busy in the sixties with both 'Lakers' and 'Salties,' that most of the time there was a small fleet of ships anchored outside the harbor, waiting for a berth to open. Salties were ocean going foreign ships, freighters, and tankers. Ships from England, France, Norway, Greece, Germany, and even China came to this most unlikely destination in the heart of the country. They carried products from their home countries, and many departed with US products destined for distant ports.

Of all the many and varied jobs Dad had, the ship

chandlery was the most memorable, interesting, and impactful to me as a child. The company was the Duluth Superior Ship Chandlery. When foreign ships arrived in port, they needed supplies. But the crew didn't hop off and go to the local grocery store. Instead, they bought everything they needed from a ship chandlery. It's a one stop shop, supplying everything from eggs to wrenches. Dad was the sales guy.

An interesting facet of the business was the three main officers of Salties who made all the purchases; Captain, Chief Engineer, and Chief Steward, each ran two sets of books. That's because they were all skimming a little off the top for themselves from the shipping company who owned the vessel. Let's say Dad sold them eggs for fifty cents a dozen. They would record sixty cents as the cost to the company, pay my the chandlery the fifty cents and pocket the ten-cent difference. Doesn't sound like much, but it added up quickly with total orders in the tens of thousands of dollars. What's more, all these transactions were done in cash. Dad would come home at night, open his briefcase, and dump piles of cash on the floor.

"Here's your allowance," he would say with a boisterous smile. There were hundred, thousand, and even five thousand-dollar bills. Remember, this was the mid-sixties. Many times, he had more money in that briefcase than what it cost to build our new house on Swan Lake Road!

The chandlery provided another service—dunnage removal and incineration. The ships had large pieces of lumber and other assorted trash from their holds, usually used to contain their cargo. Dunnage couldn't simply be dropped off at the local garbage dump. Big, bulky and dirty, the logistics of getting it off a ship and over to land efficiently and cheaply drove the business need.

DSSC bought an old steel workboat, painted it blue with a white top, and christened her the *Dolly*. My oldest brother, John, was the captain and crew. His job was simple. Navigate the *Dolly* over to the client ship, tie up on the waterside, and load the bundles of dunnage lowered down via a boom by the ship's crew. Once everything was onboard, he would head back to the chandlery's dock, where they owned a big, commercial incinerator. Everything was burned —everything.

One time, a load of fifty-gallon steel barrels came off a ship. Filled with the usual junk, Johnny dutifully took them back and dumped the contents into the incinerator. Unfortunately, Dad failed to inform him of the cases of Johnny Walker scotch that were buried at the bottoms of the barrels. He couldn't walk off the ships with that much duty-free booze or customs would have been all over him. Many times, his pants were stuffed with gifts like booze, wine, and Champagne, which had to be smuggled in. That infamous day, several cases of Europe's finest scotch went up in flames. It was a very sad day indeed.

The best part of the chandlery business for me was going to see the ships arrive and meeting the crew…the people from foreign lands. Cresting the hill on East Central Entrance, the lake, harbor, and ships came into view. Docked, anchored, arriving and departing, it was a visual and emotional transition from the quiet tranquility of the countryside to the bustle of the city. My excitement, amplified by the sheer magnitude and intrigue of these great big ships, was palpable. I loved the ships. Amazed, I couldn't imagine how something that big and heavy could float. The concept of buoyancy was beyond me at that age. It was even more intense if we were going to greet an arriving ship with friends we had made through the business—friends from distant lands across the Atlantic Ocean. The arrival date and estimated time were published in the newspaper and known by Dad as part of the chandlery business. He had a knack for timing our trips to the pier so we could see the ships approaching from the lake, down the north shore on a direct course to the port. It was a race to get to the pier before a ship entered the channel.

Down, down, down the steep hillside we would

go. Near the bottom, turn right on North Lake Avenue and over to the pier. With the station wagon barely parked, we were out and running. The two long, concrete piers boldly stood forth into Lake Superior. There was one on each side of the channel which connected the lake to the harbor. Jutting several hundred yards out, they had small lighthouses at their ends which provided navigational beacons to the incoming vessels. The two piers looked like long, outstretched arms waiting to embrace arriving ships, welcoming them back to the safety of our port. They were massive, rising high above the water with thick walls built to withstand the force and pounding of gale-driven waves… gray, frothing monsters that would routinely crash over the piers. Each pier had a protected walkway that ran right out to the very ends which protruded into the Great Lake. The ends were elevated, with stairs that lead up to pointed ends which were designed to pierce breaking waves like the bow of a ship. We would run to the end to watch the approaching ship enter the channel.

Spanning the waterway stands the Ariel Lift Bridge. Iron artwork unto itself and somewhat of an engineering masterpiece, it connects Duluth to the peninsula of Minnesota Point. It's the Point that separates the lake from the harbor. The entire span lifts horizontally straight up, allowing clearance for the ships to pass under on their way into the harbor.

It's all done through a series of cables, pulleys, and two massive, concrete counterweights driven by electric motors. It's an awesome sight to see the entire roadway lifted high up in the sky. You can actually stand right under it and watch the cars pass over through the metal grating.

Approaching ships would communicate with the bridge operator via radios, but also followed the time-honored tradition of sounding their horns. The captain would blow the ship's horn, and a few seconds later the bridge operator would reply in kind with a similar, yet distinct sounding blast from the bridge. As we stood at the end of the pier, it felt like two great steel creatures were talking to each other, while us tiny little ants watched the spectacle. No sooner had the echo of the horns bounced off the hillside and abated, than the bridge bell rang, road gates swung down, and the entire span of steel began to lift like an oversized Erector Set.

The channel waters boiled murky and dark as the Saint Louis River flows into the bay, through the harbor, and out to Lake Superior. Squeezed by the channel like putting your finger on the end of a hose, the water would accelerate. It was a bit scary to see.

The smooth concrete piers created an outflowing current so strong that anyone who fell would be pulled under and never seen again. Tragically almost every year some stupid teenagers would attempt to walk the walls of the piers during a winter gale. Huge waves coming in from the lake would crash over the piers, washing them into the channel. The currents dragged them straight under and flushed them out into the lake like ragdolls. "Bodies don't float in extremely cold water and Lake Superior is very cold," Dad would say in a sober, instructive tone. They were never found.

The power and sheer size of the ships, bridge, and water all added to the enormity of the experience. They came to life as they drew near. First the dull, low throbbing sound of their engines would cross the water to your ears. Then a mountain of water, being pushed aside by the bow, rose into a white cresting wave crashing forward under its own weight. Finally, the sight of the crew came into view, moving about the deck like ants, then stopped and began waving like crazy when they spotted us on the pier. What had first appeared as a dot on the horizon now loomed large high above us. It was like a floating skyscraper gliding through the water as it entered the channel and passed under the Ariel Lift Bridge. Mesmerized at first, we watched, then raced back down the pier trying to keep up with the passing vessel.

If the ship was fully loaded it sat low in the water. The engine noise was muffled and there was no prop wash, as the propeller was completely submersed. It would glide by almost silently. Loaded ships looked lean, fit, and elegant. Empty ships on the other hand, rode high on the water. Their exposed red hulls made them appear fat and ungainly on the water. With the engine rooms riding above the water line, and their enormous propellers breaking the surface at the top of their rotation, empty freighters were noisy and loud as they passed through the channel. Loaded or unloaded, they were always too fast for my little legs to keep up. Eventually the stern of the ship would pull away with crew members waving hello as the great ship passed under the bridge, turned left and headed toward the docks. Two blasts from the ship's horn, followed by two short blasts from the bridge, signaled they were clear, and the huge span came back down. The bells rang, gates lifted, and traffic once again crossed the boiling channel.

Now we would run back to the car and head over to the docks to welcome our friends from distant lands. Friends like Johnny Camm from England, and Helgi Moe from Norway and their ships the *Lochocra* and *Annette*. The French ships were beautiful with graceful lines, impeccably painted and decorated with a bit of artwork, and fine furniture on the officers' deck. The English kept their vessels clean, orderly and proper. The Norwegian ships were warm and homey. The Greeks ships were the exact opposite, messy, rusty, and smelly. But they were some of the most colorful, lively people we ever met. Can you say "Opa!"?

Due to Dad's chandlery business, we were always invited onboard. We thought they looked big passing through the pier but standing right next to them at the dock they looked like floating metal mountains. Gangways traversed the gap between the ship and the dock. They were nothing more than narrow, steel ladders to get on and off the ship. The steepness of the climb depended on whether the ship was fully loaded or empty. Some had handrails, but others only had a simple chain strung between metal posts which didn't lend much stability to climbing up or down. You didn't want to look down at the water sandwiched between the huge steel hull and the scarred timbers of the dock. The fear of falling was real and the risk of drowning or being crushed between the two beasts could make you freeze in place halfway up.

Once on board, our foreign friends greeted us with enthusiastic hugs and handshakes. We had become their adopted family in the States. Showered with chocolates and gifts from their homelands, we were often treated to multicourse dinners with the captains and their chiefs. The best restaurants around couldn't come close to the food or the service we received. That's where we learned what all those forks and knives were for and which ones to use first. Multiple plates, utensils and glasses came and went with each course, a far cry from heaping everything onto one large plate at home.

Even I was served a small glass of wine. Drinking wine in Europe was no big deal; it was part of their culture. But you couldn't drive a car until you were twenty-one. Personally, I think they had their priorities straight. Oh, and there was one more thing we experienced at these meals...conversation. More than eating fests, meals on the foreign ships, especially European vessels, were important experiences meant to connect, discuss, and enjoy each other's company. They were events unto themselves. We learned how to breathe before swallowing and set our forks down between bites! This really was 'foreign' territory for us, literally and figuratively.

Afterward we would be given tours of the ship from the bridge to the engine rooms. They explained how the ship worked and the purpose of all the cool things and places we saw. We were exposed to navigation, engineering, cooking, and safety. We even learned planning, though we didn't know it at the time—planning your routes, planning to feed a crew for weeks at sea, planning to have enough fuel, etc. Each deck was connected to the next by a very steep, almost vertical steel staircase. We were taught to go down backward while holding on to the railings. Again, one errant slip and fall could result in serious injury or even death. These were steel ships, with steel floors, stairs, doors, and machinery. Yet, here we were, a bunch of blond-haired little boys being treated more like adults with respect to where we could go and the things we got to touch, right down to the propeller shaft at the very bottom of the engine room. The crews were very proud of their ships and the jobs they each did regardless of their rank. We were always awestruck, and never took these tours or dinners for granted, no matter how many times we went aboard.

Our merchant marine friends loved coming out to our little farm as much as we loved going to see them. After weeks at sea crossing the Atlantic and up through the Saint Lawrence Seaway to Duluth, they wanted to spend a little time on land. Sitting in our lawn chairs, walking through the pastures, or just lying in the soft green Minnesota grass, they would tell us about their countries, towns, families, and what they did for fun. Often, they would bring fresh caught salmon from their trip and prepare great meals in Mom's humble kitchen. We never knew such culinary masterpieces could come out of our oven.

The Salties were usually only in port for a week or so. Sometimes it was only a few days to offload, load, and be on their way again. But we always packed a whole bunch of fun into their visits. When it was time to leave, we would once again drive down to the pier. This time their ships moved through the harbor with extra caution as they approached the Ariel Lift Bridge. The ship's horn would sound two blasts; the bridge would answer in kind, and up it would go.

Quietly and purposely, the great ships would pass under the bridge, through the channel, and back out into Superior. This time we would run along the pier waving and shouting goodbye to our friends heading back out to sea. The ship would give one long, last blast of its horn and the bridge responded in kind as if to say "goodbye, safe passage."

By the time we climbed the hill going home, we could barely make out the small black spot on the horizon that a few moments ago dwarfed us at the pier. If we were lucky, we might get to see them twice in one season before the lake froze over for the winter.

# ACKNOWLEDGMENTS

To my parents, John and Nancy Gilbert, who gave us the most interesting, rich, and colorful childhoods a kid could ever dream of having. To my sons, Phillip and Paul, for the honor of being your father. There has been no greater joy and purpose in my life than being your dad. And to my wife, Kathy, my soul mate…my passion. I simply could not write my stories without your unconditional love and support.

## NOTE FROM THE AUTHOR

Upon completing this book, we made a weekend trip up to Gainesville, Fl to visit my parents. Before heading back to Jupiter, I gave them a copy. When we got off the turnpike, I called to let them know we were home. They always wanted to know when we were safely off the highway. Once a parent, always a parent.

During our four-hour trip home, Dad had read it from cover to cover. He was impressed with my memory of all these stories and honored by the book. Then he put my mother on the phone. Suffering from dementia, her short-term memory gone, but long-term memories sharp as a tack. She went on and on about all the crazy stories we had from Swan Lake Road—all the fun we had. Dad had read the entire book out loud to her as she no longer reads.

That was March 3$^{rd}$, 2018. One week later, Dad collapsed on the floor. Rushed to the ER by ambulance, he was diagnosed with acute leukemia. He passed away in hospice three weeks later. My hero was gone. Mom currently lives comfortably in the memory care unit of an assisted living facility.

John Doucette Gilbert<br>
July 17, 1928-April 2, 2018<br>
Thanks Dad.

## ABOUT THE AUTHOR

Jay Gilbert grew up in the Midwest. His parents owned and operated several small businesses which took the family from Minnesota to Illinois and finally Florida. His corporate career took him and his family from Florida to Virginia, Connecticut and finally Indiana.

Between living on a farm, his many and varied business experiences, especially the family businesses including a vacuum cleaner shop, hi-fi stereos and even a motel, he has collected an eclectic inventory of experiences that are the basis for his stories.

Upon becoming Empty Nesters, he and his wife decided to move back home to Florida to be near family, especially their parents, now adult children, and grandchildren. He holds both a BSBA in Business Administration from the University of Florida and an MBA from the University of Saint Francis. An avid runner, photographer, and certifiable car nut, he is now pursuing his passion for writing. His goal is to entertain and impact even more lives through his stories. Contact the author: gilbertjay58@gmail.com

# ALSO BY JAY GILBERT

The Florida Motel: College Life - Coming of Age Romance

www.ingramcontent.com/pod-product-compliance
Lightning Source LLC
Chambersburg PA
CBHW060102230426
43661CB00033B/1397/J